ABORTION DECISIONS OF THE UNITED STATES SUPREME COURT

THE 1980'S

MAUREEN HARRISON & STEVE GILBERT
EDITORS

ABORTION DECISIONS SERIES

EXCELLENT BOOKS
BEVERLY HILLS, CALIFORNIA

EXCELLENT BOOKS
Post Office Box 7121
Beverly Hills, CA 90212-7121

Copyright © 1993 by Excellent Books. Printed in the U.S.A.

Publisher's Cataloging in Publication Data

Abortion Decisions of the United States Supreme Court: The 1980's/
  Maureen Harrison, Steve Gilbert, editors.
  p. cm. - (Abortion Decisions Series)
Bibliography:p.
Includes Index.
1. Abortion - United States, 2. Abortion - Political Aspects -
United States, 3. Abortion - Government Policy, 4. Abortion -
Law and Legislation, 5. United States Supreme Court
I. Title. II. Harrison, Maureen. III. Gilbert, Steve.
IV. Series: Abortion Decisions.
HQ767.5.U5 H24 1993 LC 92-75836
363.4'6 - dc20

ISBN 0-9628014-5-3

Introduction

On January 22, 1973, the United States Supreme Court in the landmark abortion decision, *Roe v. Wade*, found within the Fourteenth Amendment to the United States Constitution a "concept of personal liberty and restrictions upon state action . . . broad enough to emcompass a woman's decision whether or not to terminate her pregnancy."

Twenty-one times in the twenty years since the *Roe* decision the United States Supreme Court has issued major abortion decisions. The legal war of words that has resulted in challenges to and defenses of the right of women to choose abortion is the reason for the Abortion Decisions Series. This book, the second in the Abortions Decisions Series, covers the Supreme Court's eight major abortion decisions issued in the decade of the 1980's.

The tremendous personal and societal impact of the *Roe* decision, and the Supreme Court's continued upholding of that decision legalizing abortions in the United States, can be seen in the estimated number of legal abortions performed in the decade of the 1980's: 15,708,500. This estimate, based on the *Statistical Abstract of the United States* and our own interpolations, breaks down as follows:

1980	1,553,900
1981	1,577,300
1982	1,573,900
1983	1,575,000
1984	1,577,200
1985	1,588,600
1986	1,574,000
1987	1,559,100
1988	1,566,600
1989	1,562,900

The composition of the United States Supreme Court changed several times in the decade of the 1980's. In 1980 Ronald W. Reagan was elected to the first of his two terms as President of the United States. Under the U.S. Constitution it is the President, with the advice and consent of the Senate, that names Supreme Court Justices. In 1981 Justice Potter Stewart, appointed to the Court in 1958 by Dwight D. Eisenhower, retired, and was replaced by Sandra Day O'Connor, the first Reagan appointee. In 1986 Chief Justice Warren Burger, appointed to the Court in 1969 by Richard M. Nixon, retired, and was replaced by Associate Justice William Rehnquist, the second Reagan appointee. The Associate Justice seat on the Court vacated by William Rehnquist was filled in that same year by Antonin Scalia, the third Reagan appointee. In 1988 Justice Lewis Powell, Jr., appointed to the Court by Richard M. Nixon, retired, and was replaced by Anthony Kennedy, the fourth, and last, Reagan appointee.

These justices, in addition to Justices Brennan, Marshall, Blackmun, and White, made up the Court that rendered the eight major decisions in this book. For the first time, these eight decisions are presented in plain English for the general reader. In each of these carefully edited versions of the official texts issued by the Supreme Court, the editors have tried to decipher the Court's legalese without damaging or diminishing the original decision. Edited out are alpha-numeric legal citations, micro print footnotes, and wordy wrangles over points of procedure. Edited in [in brackets] are definitions [*stare decisis* = leave past decisions undisturbed], translations [*certiorari* = the decision of the Court to review a case], identifications [Appellant = Roe, Appellee = Wade], and explanations [where the case originated, how it got before the court, and who the major parties were]. You will find in this book the majority opinion of the Court as expressed by the Justice chosen to speak for the Court. All concurring and dissenting opinions of the Justices are included. A complete copy of the United States Constitution, to which all the decisions refer, follows the abortion decisions.

The Supreme Court of the United States is the court of final appeal for all legal controversies arising in the federal courts and all federal issues arising in the state courts. Only the Court has the authority to construct and interpret the meaning of the Constitution. "We are not final," wrote Justice Robert Jackson, "because we are infallible, but we are infallible because we are final." From 1857's Slavery Decision in *Dred Scott* to 1973's Abortion Decision in *Roc v. Wade*, controversy and the Court have been longtime companions.

Justice Oliver Wendell Holmes wrote: "[The Constitution] is made for people of fundamentally differing views, and the accident of our finding certain opinions natural and familiar or novel and even shocking ought not to conclude our judgment upon the question whether statutes embodying them conflict with the United States Constitution."

Those "fundamentally differing opinions" are evident in the eight major abortion decisions issued in the 1980's:

In 1980's *Harris v. McRae*, at issue is the constitutionality of publicly-funded Medicaid abortions in New York hospitals. The parties are Patricia Harris, Secretary, U.S. Department of Health & Human Services, and Cora McRae, a pregnant Medicaid recipient. The majority decision of the Court is by Justice Potter Stewart.

In 1980's *Williams v. Zbaraz*, the companion case to *Harris v. McRae*, at issue is the constitutionality of publicly-funded Medicaid abortions in Illinois. The parties are Jasper Williams, a physician, and David Zbaraz, Director, Illinois Department of Public Aid. The majority decision of the Court is by Justice Potter Stewart.

In 1981's *H.L. v. Matheson*, at issue is the constitutionality of the Utah requirements for parental consent for a minor's abortion. The parties are H.L. (the pseudonym of a pregnant minor) and Scott Matheson, Governor, Utah. The majority decision of the Court is by Chief Justice Warren Burger.

In 1983's *City of Akron v. Akron Reproductive Services*, at issue is the constitutionality of Akron, Ohio's "Regulation of Abortion" ordinance. The parties are the City of Akron, Ohio, and the Akron Center for Reproductive Health. The majority decision of the Court is by Justice Lewis Powell.

In 1983's *Planned Parenthood v. Ashcroft*, at issue is the constitutionality of the Missouri abortion statutes. The parties are Planned Parenthood of Kansas City, Missouri, and John Ashcroft, Missouri Attorney General. The majority decision of the Court is by Justice Lewis Powell.

In 1983's *Simopoulos v. Virginia* at issue is the constitutionality of Virginia's mandatory hospitalization requirement for second trimester abortions. The parties are Chris Simopoulos, an obstetrician and gynecologist, and the State of Virginia. The majority decision of the Court is by Justice Lewis Powell.

In 1986's *Thornburg v. American College*, at issue is the constitutionality of the Pennsylvania abortion law. The parties are Richard Thornburg, Governor, Pennsylvania, and the American College of Obstetricians & Gynecologists. The majority decision of the Court is by Justice Harry Blackmun.

In 1989's *Webster v. Reproductive Health Services*, at issue is the constitutionality of the Missouri abortion laws. The parties are William Webster, Attorney General, Missouri, and Reproductive Health Services. The majority decision of the Court is by Chief Justice William Rehnquist.

Judge Learned Hand wrote: "The language of the law must not be foreign to the ears of those who are to obey it." This is the second of three volumes that will reproduce in readable form the abortion decisions of the United States Supreme Court. We have tried as hard as we could, as Judge Hand urged us, to make these decisions less foreign to your ears.

M.H. & S.G.

ABOUT THE EDITORS
OF THE ABORTION DECISIONS SERIES

MAUREEN HARRISON is a textbook editor and a
member of the Supreme Court Historical Society

STEVE GILBERT is a law librarian and a member of the
American Association of Law Libraries and the
American Bar Association

Harrison & Gilbert are also the editors of:

THE LANDMARK DECISIONS SERIES

THE AMERICANS WITH DISABILITIES ACT
HANDBOOK

THE ABORTION LAW SOURCEBOOK

TABLE OF CONTENTS

AKRON v. AKRON CENTER
71

"The Court has also recognized, because abortion is a medical procedure, that the full vindication of the woman's fundamental right necessarily requires that her physician be given 'the room he needs to make his best medical judgment.' The physician's exercise of this medical judgment encompasses both assisting the woman in the decisionmaking process and implementing her decision should she choose abortion."

Justice Lewis Powell

PLANNED PARENTHOOD v. ASHCROFT
105

"In weighing the balance between protection of a woman's health and the comparatively small additional cost of a pathologist's examination, we cannot say that the Constitution requires that a State subordinate its interest in health to minimize to this extent the cost of abortions. . . ."

Justice Lewis Powell

SIMOPOULOS v. VIRGINIA
123

"We consistently have recognized and reaffirm today that a State has an 'important and legitimate interest in the health of the mother' that becomes '"compelling" . . . at approximately the end of the first trimester.'"

Justice Lewis Powell

THORNBURGH v. AMERICAN COLLEGE
135

"Few decisions are more personal and intimate, more properly private, or more basic to individual dignity and autonomy, than a woman's decision - with the guidance of her physician and within the limits specified in *Roe* - whether to end her pregnancy. A woman's right to make that choice freely is fundamental. Any other result, in our view, would protect inadequately a central part of the sphere of liberty that our law guarantees equally to all."

Justice Harry Blackmun

WEBSTER v.
REPRODUCTIVE HEALTH SERVICES
175

"Missouri's refusal to allow public employees to perform abortions in public hospitals leaves a pregnant woman with the same choices as if the State had chosen not to operate any public hospitals at all."

Justice William Rehnquist

"For today, at least, the law of abortion stands undisturbed. For today, the women of this Nation still retain the liberty to control their destinies. But the signs are evident and very ominous, and a chill wind blows."

Justice Harry Blackmun

HARRIS v. McRAE

EXCERPTS

"Regardless of whether the freedom of a woman to choose to terminate her pregnancy for health reasons lies at the core or the periphery of the due process liberty recognized in [*Roe v.*] *Wade*, it simply does not follow that a woman's freedom of choice carries with it a constitutional entitlement to the financial resources to avail herself of the full range of protected choices."

Justice Potter Stewart

"By funding all of the expenses associated with childbirth and none of the expenses incurred in terminating pregnancy, the Government literally makes an offer that the indigent woman cannot afford to refuse."

Justice William Brennan

In Brief

Question: Should Medicaid pay for abortions?

Lower Court: U.S. District Court, Eastern New York

Law: Title XIX, Social Security Act (Medicaid)
Hyde Amendment

Parties: Patricia Harris, Secretary,
Health & Human Services
Cora McRae, a pregnant Medicaid recipient

Counsel: For Harris: Wade McCree, Jr.
For McRae: Rhonda Copelon

Arguments: April 21, 1980

Decision: June 30, 1980

Majority: Chief Justice Burger, Justices Stewart, White,
Powell, Rehnquist

Minority: Justices Brennan, Marshall, Blackmun, Stevens

Decision by: Justice Stewart (p. 5)

Concurrences: Justice White (p. 18)

Dissents: Justice Brennan (p. 20)
Justice Marshall (p. 24)
Justice Blackmun (p. 30)
Justice Stevens (p. 30)

Offical Text: U.S. Reports, Vol. 488, p. 297
Lower Court: Federal Supplement, Vol. 491, p. 630

THE HARRIS COURT

Chief Justice Warren Burger
Appointed 1969 by Richard M. Nixon

Associate Justice William Brennan
Appointed 1956 by Dwight D. Eisenhower

Associate Justice Potter Stewart
Appointed 1958 by Dwight D. Eisenhower

Associate Justice Byron White
Appointed 1962 by John F. Kennedy

Associate Justice Thurgood Marshall
Appointed 1967 by Lyndon B. Johnson

Associate Justice Harry Blackmun
Appointed 1970 by Richard M. Nixon

Associate Justice Lewis Powell
Appointed 1972 by Richard M. Nixon

Associate Justice William Rehnquist
Appointed 1971 by Richard M. Nixon

Associate Justice John Paul Stevens
Appointed 1975 by Gerald R. Ford

HARRIS v. McRAE

June 30, 1980

JUSTICE STEWART: This case presents statutory and constitutional questions concerning the public funding of abortions under Title XIX of the Social Security Act, commonly known as the "Medicaid" Act, and recent annual Appropriations Acts containing the so-called "Hyde Amendment." The statutory question is whether Title XIX requires a State that participates in the Medicaid program to fund the cost of medically necessary abortions for which federal reimbursement is unavailable under the Hyde Amendment. The constitutional question, which arises only if Title XIX imposes no such requirement, is whether the Hyde Amendment, by denying public funding for certain medically necessary abortions, contravenes the liberty or equal protection guarantees of the Due Process Clause of the Fifth Amendment, or either of the Religion Clauses of the First Amendment.

The Medicaid program was created in 1965, when Congress added Title XIX to the Social Security Act, for the purpose of providing federal financial assistance to States that choose to reimburse certain costs of medical treatment for needy persons. Although participation in the Medicaid program is entirely optional, once a State elects to participate, it must comply with the requirements of Title XIX.

One such requirement is that a participating State agree to provide financial assistance to the "categorically needy" with respect to five general areas of medical treatment: (1) inpatient hospital services, (2) outpatient hospital services, (3) other laboratory and X-ray services, (4) skilled nursing facilities services, periodic screening and diagnosis of children, and family planning services, and (5) services of physicians. Although a participating State need not "provide funding for all medical treatment falling within the five general categories, [Title XIX] does require that [a] state Medicaid pla[n] establish 'reasonable standards . . . for determining . . . the extent of medical assistance under the plan which . . . are consistent with the objectives of [Title XIX].'

Since September 1976, Congress has prohibited - either by an amendment to the annual appropriations bill for the Department of Health, Education, and Welfare or by a joint resolution - the use of any federal funds to reimburse the cost of abortions under the Medicaid program except under certain specified circumstances. This funding restriction is commonly known as the "Hyde Amendment." . . . The current version of the Hyde Amendment, applicable for fiscal year 1980, provides:

"[N]one of the funds provided by this joint resolution shall be used to perform abortions except where the life of the mother would be endangered if the fetus were carried to term; or except for such medical procedures necessary for the victims of rape or incest when such rape or incest has been reported promptly to a law enforcement agency or public health service."

. . . . On September 30, 1976, the day on which Congress enacted the initial version of the Hyde Amendment, these consolidated cases [*Harris v. McRae* and *Williams v. Zbaraz*] were filed in the District Court for the Eastern District of New York. The plaintiffs - Cora McRae, a New York Medicaid recipient then in the first trimester of a pregnancy that she wished to terminate, the New York

City Health and Hospitals Corp., a public benefit corporation that operates 16 hospitals, 12 of which provide abortion services, and others - sought to enjoin [stop] the enforcement of the funding restriction on abortions. They alleged that the Hyde Amendment violated the First, Fourth, Fifth, and Ninth Amendments of the Constitution insofar as it limited the funding of abortions to those necessary to save the life of the mother, while permitting the funding of costs associated with childbirth. Although the sole named defendant was the Secretary of Health, Education, and Welfare [Patricia Harris], the District Court permitted Senators James L. Buckley and Jesse A. Helms and Representative Henry J. Hyde to intervene as defendants.

After a hearing, the District Court entered a preliminary injunction [court order] prohibiting the Secretary from enforcing the Hyde Amendment and requiring him to continue to provide federal reimbursement for abortions under the standards applicable before the funding restriction had been enacted. . . .

The Secretary then brought an appeal to this Court. After deciding *Beal v. Doe* and *Maher v. Roe*, we vacated [annulled] the injunction of the District Court and remanded [returned to the lower court] the case for reconsideration in light of those decisions.

. . . . An amended complaint was then filed, challenging the various versions of the Hyde Amendment on several grounds. At the outset, [McRae] asserted that the District Court need not address the constitutionality of the Hyde Amendment because . . . a participating State remains obligated under Title XIX to fund all medically necessary abortions, even if federal reimbursement is unavailable. With regard to the constitutionality of the Hyde Amend-

ment, [McRae] asserted, among other things, that the
funding restrictions violate the Religion Clauses of the
First Amendment and the Due Process Clause of the Fifth
Amendment.

After a lengthy trial, which inquired into the medical reasons for abortions and the diverse religious views on the
subject, the District Court filed an opinion and entered a
judgment invalidating all versions of the Hyde Amendment on constitutional grounds. The District Court . . .
conclud[ed] that even though Title XIX would otherwise
have required a participating State to fund medically necessary abortions, the Hyde Amendment had substantively
amended Title XIX to relieve a State of that funding obligation. Turning then to the constitutional issues, the District Court concluded that the Hyde Amendment, though
valid under the Establishment Clause, violates the equal
protection component of the Fifth Amendment's Due
Process Clause and the Free Exercise Clause of the First
Amendment. With regard to the Fifth Amendment, the
District Court noted that when an abortion is "medically
necessary to safeguard the pregnant woman's health, . . .
the disentitlement to [M]edicaid assistance impinges directly on the woman's right to decide, in consultation with
her physician and in reliance on his judgment, to terminate her pregnancy in order to preserve her health." The
court concluded that the Hyde Amendment violates the
equal protection guarantee because, in its view, the decision of Congress to fund medically necessary services generally but only certain medically necessary abortions
serves no legitimate governmental interest. As to the Free
Exercise Clause of the First Amendment, the court held
that insofar as a woman's decision to seek a medically necessary abortion may be a product of her religious beliefs
under certain Protestant and Jewish tenets, the funding re-

strictions of the Hyde Amendment violate that constitutional guarantee as well.

Accordingly, the District Court ordered the Secretary to "[c]ease to give effect" to the various versions of the Hyde Amendment insofar as they forbid payments for medically necessary abortions. It further directed the Secretary to "[c]ontinue to authorize the expenditure of federal matching funds [for such abortions]." ...

The Secretary then applied to this Court for a stay [suspension] of the judgment pending direct appeal of the District Court's decision. We denied the stay, but [agreed to hear] this appeal.

. . . . Accordingly, we turn first to the question whether Title XIX requires a State that participates in the Medicaid program to continue to fund those medically necessary abortions for which federal reimbursement is unavailable under the Hyde Amendment. If a participating State is under such an obligation, the constitutionality of the Hyde Amendment need not be drawn into question in the present case, for the availability of medically necessary abortions under Medicaid would continue, with the participating State shouldering the total cost of funding such abortions.

. . . . The Medicaid program created by Title XIX is a cooperative endeavor in which the Federal Government provides financial assistance to participating States to aid them in furnishing health care to needy persons. Under this system of "cooperative federalism," if a State agrees to establish a Medicaid plan that satisfies the requirements of Title XIX, which include several mandatory categories of health services, the Federal Government agrees to pay a specified percentage of "the total amount expended . . . as medical assistance under the State plan. The cornerstone of Medicaid is financial contribution by both the Federal Government and the participating State. Nothing in Title XIX as originally enacted, or in its legislative history, suggests that Congress intended to require a participating State to assume the full costs of providing any health services in its Medicaid plan. Quite the contrary, the purpose of Congress in enacting Title XIX was to provide federal financial assistance for all legitimate state expenditures under an approved Medicaid plan.

Since the Congress that enacted Title XIX did not intend a participating State to assume a unilateral funding obligation for any health service in an approved Medicaid plan, it follows that Title XIX does not require a participating State to include in its plan any services for which a subsequent Congress has withheld federal funding. . . . [I]f Congress chooses to withdraw federal funding for a particular service, a State is not obliged to continue to pay for that service as a condition of continued federal financial support of other services. . . .

Thus, by the normal operation of Title XIX, even if a State were otherwise required to include medically necessary abortions in its Medicaid plan, the withdrawal of federal funding under the Hyde Amendment would operate to relieve the State of that obligation for those abortions for which federal reimbursement is unavailable. . . . Accordingly, we conclude that Title XIX does not require a participating State to pay for those medically necessary abortions for which federal reimbursement is unavailable under the Hyde Amendment.

Having determined that Title XIX does not obligate a participating State to pay for those medically necessary abortions for which Congress has withheld federal funding, we must consider the constitutional validity of the Hyde Amendment. [McRae] assert[s] that the funding restrictions of the Hyde Amendment violate several rights secured by the Constitution - (1) the right of a woman, implicit in the Due Process Clause of the Fifth Amendment, to decide whether to terminate a pregnancy, (2) the prohibition under the Establishment Clause of the First Amendment against any "law respecting an establishment of religion," and (3) the right to freedom of religion protected by the Free Exercise Clause of the First Amendment. [McRae] also contend[s] that . . . the Hyde Amendment violates the equal protection component of the Fifth Amendment.

It is well settled that, quite apart from the guarantee of equal protection, if a law "impinges upon a fundamental right explicitly or implicitly secured by the Constitution [it] is presumptively unconstitutional." Accordingly, before turning to the equal protection issue in this case, we examine whether the Hyde Amendment violates any substantive rights secured by the Constitution.

. . . . In the [Roe v.] Wade case, this Court held unconstitutional a Texas statute making it a crime to procure or attempt an abortion except on medical advice for the purpose of saving the mother's life. The constitutional underpinning of [Roe v.] Wade was a recognition that the "liberty" protected by the Due Process Clause of the Fourteenth Amendment includes not only the freedoms explicitly mentioned in the Bill of Rights, but also a freedom of personal choice in certain matters of marriage and family life. This implicit constitutional liberty, the Court in [Roe v.] *Wade* held, includes the freedom of a woman to decide whether to terminate a pregnancy.

But the Court in [*Roe v.*] *Wade* also recognized that a State has legitimate interests during a pregnancy in both ensuring the health of the mother and protecting potential human life. These state interests, which were found to be "separate and distinct" and to "gro[w] in substantiality as the woman approaches term," pose a conflict with a woman's untrammeled freedom of choice. In resolving this conflict, the Court held that before the end of the first trimester of pregnancy, neither state interest is sufficiently substantial to justify any intrusion on the woman's freedom of choice. In the second trimester, the state interest in maternal health was found to be sufficiently substantial to justify regulation reasonably related to that concern. And at viability, usually in the third trimester, the state interest in protecting the potential life of the fetus was found to justify a criminal prohibition against abortions, except where necessary for the preservation of the life or health of the mother. Thus, inasmuch as the Texas criminal statute allowed abortions only where necessary to save the life of the mother and without regard to the stage of the pregnancy, the Court held in [*Roe v.*] *Wade* that the statute violated the Due Process Clause of the Fourteenth Amendment.

In *Maher v. Roe*, the Court was presented with the question whether the scope of personal constitutional freedom recognized in *Roe v. Wade* included an entitlement to Medicaid payments for abortions that are not medically necessary. At issue in *Maher* was a Connecticut welfare regulation under which Medicaid recipients received payments for medical services incident to childbirth, but not for medical services incident to nontherapeutic abortions. . . .

The doctrine of *Roe v. Wade*, the Court held in *Maher*, "protects the woman from unduly burdensome interference with her freedom to decide whether to terminate her pregnancy," such as the severe criminal sanctions at issue in *Roe v. Wade*, or the absolute requirement of spousal consent for an abortion challenged in *Planned Parenthood of Central Missouri v. Danforth*.

But the constitutional freedom recognized in [*Roe v.*] *Wade* and its progeny, the *Maher* Court explained, did not prevent Connecticut from making "a value judgment favoring childbirth over abortion, and . . . implement[ing] that judgment by the allocation of public funds." . . .

In explaining why the constitutional principle recognized in [*Roe v.*] *Wade* and later cases - protecting a woman's freedom of choice - did not translate into a constitutional obligation of Connecticut to subsidize abortions, the Court cited the "basic difference between direct state interference with a protected activity and state encouragement of an alternative activity consonant with legislative policy." . . . [E]ven though the Connecticut regulation favored childbirth over abortion by means of subsidization of one and not the other, the Court in *Maher* concluded that the regulation did not impinge on the constitutional freedom recognized in [*Roe v.*] *Wade* because it imposed no governmental restriction on access to abortions.

The Hyde Amendment, like the Connecticut welfare regulation at issue in *Maher*, places no governmental obstacle in the path of a woman who chooses to terminate her pregnancy, but rather, by means of unequal subsidization of abortion and other medical services, encourages alternative activity deemed in the public interest. . . . It is the [McRae's] view that to the extent that the Hyde Amendment withholds funding for certain medically necessary abortions, it clearly impinges on the constitutional principle recognized in [*Roe v.*] *Wade.*

It is evident that a woman's interest in protecting her health was an important theme in [*Roe v.*] *Wade.* In concluding that the freedom of a woman to decide whether to terminate her pregnancy falls within the personal liberty protected by the Due Process Clause, the Court in [*Roe v.*] *Wade* emphasized the fact that the woman's decision carries with it significant personal health implications - both physical and psychological. . . . Because even the compelling interest of the State in protecting potential life after fetal viability was held to be insufficient to outweigh a woman's decision to protect her life or health, it could be argued that the freedom of a woman to decide whether to terminate her pregnancy for health reasons does in fact lie at the core of the constitutional liberty identified in [*Roe v.*] *Wade.*

But, regardless of whether the freedom of a woman to choose to terminate her pregnancy for health reasons lies at the core or the periphery of the due process liberty recognized in [*Roe v.*] *Wade,* it simply does not follow that a woman's freedom of choice carries with it a constitutional entitlement to the financial resources to avail herself of the full range of protected choices. The reason why was explained in *Maher:* although government may not place obstacles in the path of a woman's exercise of her freedom of choice, it need not remove those not of its own creation. Indigency falls in the latter category. . . . Although Congress has opted to subsidize medically neces-

sary services generally, but not certain medically necessary abortions, the fact remains that the Hyde Amendment leaves an indigent woman with at least the same
range of choice in deciding whether to obtain a medically
necessary abortion as she would have had if Congress had
chosen to subsidize no health care costs at all. We are
thus not persuaded that the Hyde Amendment impinges
on the constitutionally protected freedom of choice recognized in [*Roe v.*] *Wade.*

Although the liberty protected by the Due Process Clause
affords protection against unwarranted government interference with freedom of choice in the context of certain
personal decisions, it does not confer an entitlement to
such funds as may be necessary to realize all the advan-
tages of that freedom. To hold otherwise would mark
a drastic change in our understanding of the Constitution. . . . To translate the limitation on governmental
power implicit in the Due Process Clause into an affirmative funding obligation would require Congress to subsidize the medically necessary abortion of an indigent woman even if Congress had not enacted a Medicaid program
to subsidize other medically necessary services. Nothing
in the Due Process Clause supports such an extraordinary
result. Whether freedom of choice that is constitutionally
protected warrants federal subsidization is a question for
Congress to answer, not a matter of constitutional entitlement. Accordingly, we conclude that the Hyde Amendment does not impinge on the due process liberty recognized in [*Roe v.*] *Wade.*

.... It is the [McRae's] view that the Hyde Amendment
violates the Establishment Clause because it incorporates
into law the doctrines of the Roman Catholic Church concerning the sinfulness of abortion and the time at which

life commences. Moreover, insofar as a woman's decision to seek a medically necessary abortion may be a product of her religious beliefs under certain Protestant and Jewish tenets, [McRae] assert[s] that the funding limitations of the Hyde Amendment impinge on the freedom of religion guaranteed by the Free Exercise Clause.

. . . . [T]he District Court properly concluded that the Hyde Amendment does not run afoul of the Establishment Clause. . . . The Hyde Amendment, as the District Court noted, is as much a reflection of "traditionalist" values towards abortion, as it is an embodiment of the views of any particular religion. . . . [W]e are convinced that the fact that the funding restrictions in the Hyde Amendment may coincide with the religious tenets of the Roman Catholic Church does not, without more, contravene the Establishment Clause.

. . . . It remains to be determined whether the Hyde Amendment violates the equal protection component of the Fifth Amendment. This challenge is premised on the fact that, although federal reimbursement is available under Medicaid for medically necessary services generally, the Hyde Amendment does not permit federal reimbursement of all medically necessary abortions. . . .

Here, as in *Maher*, the principal impact of the Hyde Amendment falls on the indigent. But that fact does not itself render the funding restriction constitutionally invalid. . . .

The remaining question then is whether the Hyde Amendment is rationally related to a legitimate government objective. . . .

[T]he Hyde Amendment, by encouraging childbirth except in the most urgent circumstances, is rationally related to the legitimate governmental objective of protecting potential life. By subsidizing the medical expenses of indigent women who carry their pregnancies to term while not subsidizing the comparable expenses of women who undergo abortions (except those whose lives are threatened), Congress has established incentives that make childbirth a more attractive alternative than abortion for persons eligible for Medicaid. These incentives bear a direct relationship to the legitimate congressional interest in protecting potential life. . . . Abortion is inherently different from other medical procedures, because no other procedure involves the purposeful termination of a potential life.

. . . . It is the role of the courts only to ensure that congressional decisions comport with the Constitution.

Where, as here, the Congress has neither invaded a substantive constitutional right or freedom, nor enacted legislation that purposefully operates to the detriment of a suspect class, the only requirement of equal protection is that congressional action be rationally related to a legitimate governmental interest. The Hyde Amendment satisfies that standard. It is not the mission of this Court or any other to decide whether the balance of competing interests reflected in the Hyde Amendment is wise social policy. If that were our mission, not every Justice who has subscribed to the judgment of the Court today could have done so. But we cannot, in the name of the Constitution, overturn duly enacted statutes simply "because they may be unwise, improvident, or out of harmony with a particular school of thought." Rather, "when an issue involves policy choices as sensitive as those implicated

[here] . . . , the appropriate forum for their resolution in a democracy is the legislature."

For the reasons stated in this opinion, we hold that a State that participates in the Medicaid program is not obligated under Title XIX to continue to fund those medically necessary abortions for which federal reimbursement is unavailable under the Hyde Amendment. We further hold that the funding restrictions of the Hyde Amendment violate neither the Fifth Amendment nor the Establishment Clause of the First Amendment. . . . Accordingly, the judgment of the District Court is reversed, and the case is remanded [returned] to that court for further proceedings consistent with this opinion.

It is so ordered.

JUSTICE WHITE, concurring: I join the Court's opinion and judgment with these additional remarks.

Roe v. Wade held that prior to viability of the fetus, the governmental interest in potential life was insufficient to justify overriding the due process right of a pregnant woman to terminate her pregnancy by abortion. In the last trimester, however, the State's interest in fetal life was deemed sufficiently strong to warrant a ban on abortions, but only if continuing the pregnancy did not threaten the life or health of the mother. In the latter event, the State was required to respect the choice of the mother to terminate her pregnancy and protect her health.

. . . . The constitutional right recognized in *Roe v. Wade* was the right to choose to undergo an abortion without coercive interference by the government. As the Court points out, *Roe v. Wade* did not purport to adjudicate a right to have abortions funded by the government, but only to be free from unreasonable official interference with private choice. . . .

Roe v. Wade . . . dealt with the circumstances in which the governmental interest in potential life would justify official interference with the abortion choices of pregnant women. There is no such calculus involved here. The Government does not seek to interfere with or to impose any coercive restraint on the choice of any woman to have an abortion. The woman's choice remains unfettered, the Government is not attempting to use its interest in life to justify a coercive restraint, and hence in disbursing its Medicaid funds it is free to implement rationally what *Roe v. Wade* recognized to be its legitimate interest in a potential life by covering the medical costs of childbirth but denying funds for abortions. Neither *Roe v. Wade* nor any of the cases decided in its wake invalidates this legislative preference. . . .

Maher held that the government need not fund elective abortions because withholding funds rationally furthered the State's legitimate interest in normal childbirth. We sustained [approved] this policy even though under *Roe v. Wade*, the government's interest in fetal life is an inadequate justification for coercive interference with the pregnant woman's right to choose an abortion, whether or not such a procedure is medically indicated. We have already held, therefore, that the interest balancing involved in *Roe v. Wade* is not controlling in resolving the present constitutional issue. Accordingly, I am satisfied that the straightforward analysis followed in Justice Stewart's opinion for the Court is sound.

JUSTICE BRENNAN (joined by Justices Marshall and Blackmun), dissenting [This opinion also applies to *Williams v. Zbaraz*]: . . . . [T]he State's interest in protecting the potential life of the fetus cannot justify the exclusion of financially and medically needy women from the benefits to which they would otherwise be entitled solely because the treatment that a doctor has concluded is medically necessary involves an abortion. I write separately to express my continuing disagreement with the Court's mischaracterization of the nature of the fundamental right recognized in *Roe v. Wade* and its misconception of the manner in which that right is infringed by federal and state legislation withdrawing all funding for medically necessary abortions.

Roe v. Wade held that the constitutional right to personal privacy encompasses a woman's decision whether or not to terminate her pregnancy. *Roe* and its progeny established that the pregnant woman has a right to be free from state interference with her choice to have an abortion - a right which, at least prior to the end of the first trimester, absolutely prohibits any governmental regulation of that highly personal decision. The proposition for which these cases stand thus is not that the State is under an affirmative obligation to ensure access to abortions for all who may desire them; it is that the State must refrain from wielding its enormous power and influence in a manner that might burden the pregnant woman's freedom to choose whether to have an abortion. The Hyde Amendment's denial of public funds for medically necessary abortions plainly intrudes upon this constitutionally protected decision, for both by design and in effect it serves to coerce indigent pregnant women to bear children that they would otherwise elect not to have.

When viewed in the context of the Medicaid program to which it is appended, it is obvious that the Hyde Amendment is nothing less than an attempt by Congress to circumvent the dictates of the Constitution and achieve indirectly what *Roe v. Wade* said it could not do directly. Under Title XIX of the Social Security Act, the Federal Government reimburses participating States for virtually all medically necessary services it provides to the categorically needy. The sole limitation of any significance is the Hyde Amendment's prohibition against the use of any federal funds to pay for the costs of abortions (except where the life of the mother would be endangered if the fetus were carried to term). . . . [E]xclusion of medically necessary abortions from Medicaid coverage cannot be justified as a cost-saving device. Rather, the Hyde Amendment is a transparent attempt by the Legislative Branch to impose the political majority's judgment of the morally acceptable and socially desirable preference on a sensitive and intimate decision that the Constitution entrusts to the individual. Worse yet, the Hyde Amendment does not foist that majoritarian viewpoint with equal measure upon everyone in our Nation, rich and poor alike; rather, it imposes that viewpoint only upon that segment of our society which, because of its position of political powerlessness, is least able to defend its privacy rights from the encroachments of state-mandated morality. . . . Though it may not be this Court's mission "to decide whether the balance of competing interests reflected in the Hyde Amendment is wise social policy," it most assuredly is our responsibility to vindicate the pregnant woman's constitutional right to decide whether to bear children free from governmental intrusion.

Moreover, it is clear that the Hyde Amendment not only was designed to inhibit, but does in fact inhibit the woman's freedom to choose abortion over childbirth. . . . In every pregnancy [abortion or childbirth] is medically necessary, and the poverty-stricken woman depends on the Medicaid Act to pay for the expenses associated with that procedure. But under the Hyde Amendment, the Government will fund only those procedures incidental to childbirth. By thus injecting coercive financial incentives favoring childbirth into a decision that is constitutionally guaranteed to be free from governmental intrusion, the Hyde Amendment deprives the indigent woman of her freedom to choose abortion over maternity, thereby impinging on the due process liberty recognized in *Roe v. Wade*.

The Court's contrary conclusion is premised on its belief that "[t]he financial constraints that restrict an indigent woman's ability to enjoy the full range of constitutionally protected freedom of choice are the product not of governmental restrictions on access to abortions, but rather of her indigency." Accurate as this statement may be, it reveals only half the picture. For what the Court fails to appreciate is that it is not simply the woman's indigency that interferes with her freedom of choice, but the combination of her own poverty and the Government's unequal subsidization of abortion and childbirth.

. . . . By funding all of the expenses associated with childbirth and none of the expenses incurred in terminating pregnancy, the Government literally makes an offer that the indigent woman cannot afford to refuse. It matters not that in this instance the Government has used the carrot rather than the stick. What is critical is the realization that as a practical matter, many poverty-stricken women will choose to carry their pregnancy to term simply because the Government provides funds for the associated medical services, even though these same women would have chosen to have an abortion if the Government had also paid for that option, or indeed if the Government had stayed out of the picture altogether and had defrayed the costs of neither procedure.

The fundamental flaw in the Court's due process analysis, then, is its failure to acknowledge that the discriminatory distribution of the benefits of governmental largesse can discourage the exercise of fundamental liberties just as effectively as can an outright denial of those rights through criminal and regulatory sanctions. Implicit in the Court's reasoning is the notion that as long as the Government is not obligated to provide its citizens with certain benefits or privileges, it may condition the grant of such benefits on the recipient's relinquishment of his constitutional rights.

. . . . [W]e have heretofore never hesitated to invalidate any scheme of granting or withholding financial benefits that incidentally or intentionally burdens one manner of exercising a constitutionally protected choice. . . .

The Medicaid program cannot be distinguished from these other statutory schemes that unconstitutionally burdened fundamental rights. . . . [T]he government withholds financial benefits in a manner that discourages the exercise of a due process liberty: The indigent woman who chooses to assert her constitutional right to have an abortion can do so only on pain of sacrificing health-care benefits to which she would otherwise be entitled. . . .

I respectfully dissent.

JUSTICE MARSHALL, dissenting [This opinion also applies to *Williams v. Zbaraz*]: Three years ago, in *Maher v. Roe*, the Court upheld a state program that excluded nontherapeutic abortions from a welfare program that generally subsidized the medical expenses incidental to pregnancy and childbirth. At that time, I expressed my fear "that the Court's decisions will be an invitation to public officials, already under extraordinary pressure from well-financed and carefully orchestrated lobbying campaigns, to approve more such restrictions" on governmental funding for abortion.

That fear has proved justified. Under the Hyde Amendment, federal funding is denied for abortions that are medically necessary and that are necessary to avert severe and permanent damage to the health of the mother. The Court's opinion studiously avoids recognizing the undeniable fact that for women eligible for Medicaid - poor women - denial of a Medicaid-funded abortion is equivalent to denial of legal abortion altogether. By definition, these women do not have the money to pay for an abortion themselves. If abortion is medically necessary and a funded abortion is unavailable, they must resort to back-alley butchers, attempt to induce an abortion themselves by crude and dangerous methods, or suffer the serious medical consequences of attempting to carry the fetus to term. Because legal abortion is not a realistic option for such women, the predictable result of the Hyde Amendment will be a significant increase in the number of poor women who will die or suffer significant health damage because of an inability to procure necessary medical services.

The legislation before us is the product of an effort to deny to the poor the constitutional right recognized in

Roe v. Wade, even though the cost may be serious and long-lasting health damage. . . . The denial of Medicaid benefits to individuals who meet all the statutory criteria for eligibility, solely because the treatment that is medically necessary involves the exercise of the fundamental right to choose abortion, is a form of discrimination repugnant to the equal protection of the laws guaranteed by the Constitution. The Court's decision today marks a retreat from *Roe v. Wade* and represents a cruel blow to the most powerless members of our society. I dissent.

. . . . Federal funding is . . . unavailable [under the Hyde Amendment] even when severe and long-lasting health damage to the mother is a virtual certainty. Nor are federal funds available when severe health damage, or even death, will result to the fetus if it is carried to term.

The record developed [in the court] below reveals that the standards set forth in the Hyde Amendment exclude the majority of cases in which the medical profession would recommend abortion as medically necessary. Indeed, in States that have adopted a standard more restrictive than the "medically necessary" test of the Medicaid Act, the number of funded abortions has decreased by over 98%.

The impact of the Hyde Amendment on indigent women falls into four major categories. First, the Hyde Amendment prohibits federal funding for abortions that are necessary in order to protect the health and sometimes the life of the mother. . . .

Second, federal funding is denied in cases in which severe mental disturbances will be created by unwanted pregnancies. . . .

Third, the Hyde Amendment denies funding for the majority of women whose pregnancies have been caused by rape or incest. . . .

Finally, federal funding is unavailable in cases in which it is known that the fetus itself will be unable to survive. . . .

An optimistic estimate indicates that as many as 100 excess deaths may occur each year as a result of the Hyde Amendment. The record contains no estimate of the health damage that may occur to poor women, but it shows that it will be considerable.

. . . . I continue to believe that the rigid "two-tiered" approach is inappropriate and that the Constitution requires a more exacting standard of review than mere rationality in cases such as this one. Further, in my judgment the Hyde Amendment cannot pass constitutional muster even under the rational-basis standard of review.

. . . . With all deference, I am unable to understand how the Court can afford the same level of scrutiny to the legislation involved here - whose cruel impact falls exclusively on indigent pregnant women - that it has given to legislation distinguishing opticians from opthalmologists, or to other legislation that makes distinctions between economic interests more than able to protect themselves in the political process. Heightened scrutiny of legislative classifications has always been designed to protect groups "saddled with such disabilities, or subjected to such a history of purposeful unequal treatment, or relegated to such a position of political powerlessness as to command extraordinary protection from the majoritarian political process." And while it is now clear that traditional "strict scrutiny" is unavailable to protect the poor against classifications that disfavor them, I do not believe that legislation that imposes a crushing burden on indigent women can be treated with the same deference given to legislation distinguishing among business interests.

The Hyde Amendment, of course, distinguishes between medically necessary abortions and other medically necessary expenses. . . .

An indigent woman denied governmental funding for a medically necessary abortion is confronted with two grotesque choices. First, she may seek to obtain "an illegal abortion that poses a serious threat to her health and even her life." Alternatively, she may attempt to bear the child, a course that may both significantly threaten her health and eliminate any chance she might have had "to control the direction of her own life."

The class burdened by the Hyde Amendment consists of indigent women, a substantial proportion of whom are members of minority races. . . . I continue to believe that "a showing that state action has a devastating impact on the lives of minority racial groups must be relevant" for purposes of equal protection analysis.

. . . . I am unable to see how even a minimally rational legislature could conclude that the interest in fetal life outweighs the brutal effect of the Hyde Amendment on indigent women. Moreover, both the legislation in *Maher* and the Hyde Amendment were designed to deprive poor and minority women of the constitutional right to choose abortion. That purpose is not constitutionally permitted under *Roe v. Wade.*

.... [T]he Hyde Amendment is a denial of equal protection. ...

Under Title XIX and the Hyde Amendment, funding is available for essentially all necessary medical treatment for the poor. [McRae] ha[s] met the statutory requirements for eligibility, but [is] excluded because the treatment that is medically necessary involves the exercise of a fundamental right, the right to choose an abortion. In short, [McRae] ha[s] been deprived of a governmental benefit for which [she is] otherwise eligible, solely because [she] ha[s] attempted to exercise a constitutional right. The interest asserted by the Government, the protection of fetal life, has been declared constitutionally subordinate to [McRae's] interest in preserving [her] li[fe] and health by obtaining medically necessary treatment. And finally, the purpose of the legislation was to discourage the exercise of the fundamental right. In such circumstances the Hyde Amendment must be invalidated because it does not meet even the rational-basis standard of review.

The consequences of today's opinion - consequences to which the Court seems oblivious - are not difficult to predict. Pregnant women denied the funding necessary to procure abortions will be restricted to two alternatives. First, they can carry the fetus to term - even though that route may result in severe injury or death to the mother, the fetus, or both. If that course appears intolerable, they can resort to self-induced abortions or attempt to obtain illegal abortions - not because bearing a child would be inconvenient, but because it is necessary in order to protect their health. The result will not be to protect what the Court describes as "the legitimate governmental objective of protecting potential life," but to ensure the destruction of both fetal and maternal life. "There is another world 'out there,' the existence of which the Court . . . either chooses to ignore or fears to recognize." In my view, it is only by blinding itself to that other world that the Court can reach the result it announces today.

Ultimately, the result reached today may be traced to the Court's unwillingness to apply the constraints of the Constitution to decisions involving the expenditure of governmental funds. In today's decision, as in *Maher v. Roe*, the Court suggests that a withholding of funding imposes no real obstacle to a woman deciding whether to exercise her constitutionally protected procreative choice, even though the Government is prepared to fund all other medically necessary expenses, including the expenses of childbirth. The Court perceives this result as simply a distinction between a "limitation on governmental power" and "an affirmative funding obligation." For a poor person attempting to exercise her "right" to freedom of choice, the difference is imperceptible. . . . [T]he differential distribution of incentives - which the Court concedes is present here - can have precisely the same effect as an outright prohibition. It is no more sufficient an answer here than it was in *Roe v. Wade* to say that "'the appropriate forum'" for the resolution of sensitive policy choices is the legislature.

More than 35 years ago, Justice Jackson observed that the "task of translating the majestic generalities of the Bill of Rights . . . into concrete restraints on officials dealing with the problems of the twentieth century is one to disturb self-confidence." . . .

In this case, the Federal Government has taken upon itself the burden of financing practically all medically necessary expenditures. One category of medically necessary expenditure has been singled out for exclusion, and the sole basis for the exclusion is a premise repudiated for purposes of constitutional law in *Roe v. Wade.* The consequence is a devastating impact on the lives and health of poor women. I do not believe that a Constitution committed to the equal protection of the laws can tolerate this result. I dissent.

JUSTICE BLACKMUN, dissenting [This opinion also applies to *Williams v. Zbaraz*]: . . . . There is "condescension" in the Court's holding that "she may go elsewhere for her abortion"; this is "disingenuous and alarming"; the Government "punitively impresses upon a needy minority its own concepts of the socially desirable, the publicly acceptable, and the morally sound"; the "financial argument, of course, is specious"; there truly is "another world 'out there,' the existence of which the Court, I suspect, either chooses to ignore or fears to recognize"; the "cancer of poverty will continue to grow"; and "the lot of the poorest among us, once again, and still, is not to be bettered."

JUSTICE STEVENS, dissenting [This opinion also applies to *Williams v. Zbaraz*]: "The federal sovereign, like the States, must govern impartially. The concept of equal justice under law is served by the Fifth Amendment's guarantee of due process, as well as by the Equal Protection Clause of the Fourteenth Amendment." When the sovereign provides a special benefit or a special protection for a class of persons, it must define the membership in the class by neutral criteria; it may not make special exceptions for reasons that are constitutionally insufficient.

These cases [*Harris v. McRae* and *Williams v. Zbaraz*] involve the pool of benefits that Congress created by enacting Title XIX of the Social Security Act in 1965. Individuals who satisfy two neutral statutory criteria - financial
need and medical need - are entitled to equal access to
that pool. The question is whether certain persons who
satisfy those criteria may be denied access to benefits solely because they must exercise the constitutional right to
have an abortion in order to obtain the medical care they
need. Our prior cases plainly dictate the answer to that
question.

A fundamentally different question was decided in *Maher
v. Roe.* Unlike [McRae], the [plaintiff] in *Maher* [Roe]
did not satisfy the neutral criterion of medical need; [she]
sought a subsidy for nontherapeutic abortions - medical
procedures which by definition [she] did not need. In rejecting that claim, the Court held that [her] constitutional
right to choose that procedure did not impose a duty on
the State to subsidize the exercise of that right. Nor did
the fact that the State had undertaken to pay for the necessary medical care associated with childbirth require the
State also to pay for abortions that were not necessary;
for only necessary medical procedures satisfied the neutral statutory criteria. Nontherapeutic abortions were
simply outside the ambit of the medical benefits program.
Thus, in *Maher,* [Roe's] desire to exercise a constitutional
right gave rise to neither special access nor special exclusion from the pool of benefits created by Title XIX.

These cases involve a special exclusion of women who, by
definition, are confronted with a choice between two serious harms: serious health damage to themselves on the
one hand and abortion on the other. The competing interests are the interest in maternal health and the interest in

protecting potential human life. It is now part of our law
that the pregnant woman's decision as to which of these
conflicting interests shall prevail is entitled to constitutional protection.

In *Roe v. Wade* and *Doe v. Bolton*, . . . the Court held that
a woman's freedom to elect to have an abortion prior to
viability has absolute constitutional protection, subject
only to valid health regulations. . . .

If a woman has a constitutional right to place a higher
value on avoiding either serious harm to her own health
or perhaps an abnormal childbirth than on protecting potential life, the exercise of that right cannot provide the
basis for the denial of a benefit to which she would otherwise be entitled. The Court's sterile equal protection
analysis evades this critical though simple point. . . . [I]t
is misleading to speak of the Government's legitimate interest in the fetus without reference to the context in
which that interest was held to be legitimate. . . . It is . . .
perfectly clear that neither the Federal Government nor
the States may exclude a woman from medical benefits to
which she would otherwise be entitled solely to further an
interest in potential life when a physician, "in appropriate
medical judgment," certifies that an abortion is necessary
"for the preservation of the life or health of the mother."
The Court totally fails to explain why this reasoning is
not dispositive here.

It cannot be denied that the harm inflicted upon women
in the excluded class is grievous. As the Court's compari-
son of the differing forms of the Hyde Amendment that
have been enacted since 1976 demonstrates, the Court expressly approves the exclusion of benefits in "instances
where severe and long-lasting physical health damage to

the mother" is the predictable consequence of carrying the pregnancy to term. . . . Because a denial of benefits for medically necessary abortions inevitably causes serious harm to the excluded women, it is tantamount to severe punishment. In my judgment, that denial cannot be justified unless government may, in effect, punish women who want abortions. But as the Court unequivocally held in *Roe v. Wade*, this the government may not do.

Nor can it be argued that the exclusion of this type of medically necessary treatment of the indigent can be justified on fiscal grounds. There are some especially costly forms of treatment that may reasonably be excluded from the program in order to preserve the assets in the pool and extend its benefits to the maximum number of needy persons. Fiscal considerations may compel certain difficult choices in order to improve the protection afforded to the entire benefited class. But, ironically, the exclusion of medically necessary abortions harms the entire class as well as its specific victims. . . . [T]he decision to tolerate harm to indigent persons who need an abortion in order to avoid "serious and long-lasting health damage" is one that is financed by draining money out of the pool that is used to fund all other necessary medical procedures. Unlike most invidious classifications, this discrimination harms not only its direct victims but also the remainder of the class of needy persons that the pool was designed to benefit.

. . . . Having decided to alleviate some of the hardships of poverty by providing necessary medical care, the government must use neutral criteria in distributing benefits. It may not deny benefits to a financially and medically needy person simply because he is a Republication, a Catholic, or an Oriental - or because he has spoken against a program the government has a legitimate interest in furthering. In sum, it may not create exceptions for the sole purpose of furthering a governmental interest that is constitutionally subordinate to the individual interest that the entire program was designed to protect. The Hyde Amendments not only exclude financially and medically needy persons from the pool of benefits for a constitutionally insufficient reason; they also require the expenditure of millions and millions of dollars in order to thwart the exercise of a constitutional right, thereby effectively inflicting serious and long-lasting harm on impoverished women who want and need abortions for valid medical reasons. In my judgment, these Amendments constitute an unjustifiable, and indeed blatant, violation of the sovereign's duty to govern impartially.

I respectfully dissent.

WILLIAMS v. ZBARAZ

EXCERPTS

"[A] participating State is not obligated under Title XIX [Medicaid] to pay for those medically necessary abortions for which federal reimbursement is unavailable. . . ."

Justice Potter Stewart

"The Court's opinion studiously avoids recognizing the undeniable fact that for women eligible for Medicaid - poor women - denial of a Medicaid-funded abortion is equivalent to denial of legal abortion altogether."

Justice Thurgood Marshall

In Brief

Question: Is the Illinois abortion law constitutional?

Lower Court: U.S. District Court, Northern Illinois

Law: Illinois Revised Statute, Chapter 23 (1929)
Title XIX, Social Security Act (Medicaid)
Hyde Amendment

Parties: Jasper Williams, a physician
David Zbaraz, Director,
Illinois Department of Public Aid

Counsel: For Williams: Victor Rosenblum
For Zbaraz: Robert Bennett

Arguments: April 21, 1980

Decision: June 30, 1980

Majority: Chief Justice Burger, Justices Stewart, White,
Powell, Rehnquist

Minority: Justices Brennan, Marshall, Blackmun, Stevens

Decision by: Justice Stewart (p. 39)

Dissents: Justice Brennan (see *Harris v. McRae*, p. 20)
Justice Marshall (see *Harris v. McRae*,
p. 24)
Justice Blackmun (see *Harris v. McRae*,
p. 30)
Justice Stevens (see *Harris v. McRae*, p. 30)

Offical Text: U.S. Reports, Vol. 448, p. 358
Lower Court: Federal Supplement, Vol. 469, p. 1212

THE WILLIAMS COURT

Chief Justice Warren Burger
Appointed 1969 by Richard M. Nixon

Associate Justice William Brennan
Appointed 1956 by Dwight D. Eisenhower

Associate Justice Potter Stewart
Appointed 1958 by Dwight D. Eisenhower

Associate Justice Byron White
Appointed 1962 by John F. Kennedy

Associate Justice Thurgood Marshall
Appointed 1967 by Lyndon B. Johnson

Associate Justice Harry Blackmun
Appointed 1970 by Richard M. Nixon

Associate Justice Lewis Powell
Appointed 1972 by Richard M. Nixon

Associate Justice William Rehnquist
Appointed 1971 by Richard M. Nixon

Associate Justice John Paul Stevens
Appointed 1975 by Gerald R. Ford

WILLIAMS v. ZBARAZ

June 30, 1980

JUSTICE STEWART: This suit was brought . . . in the District Court for the Northern District of Illinois to enjoin [stop] the enforcement of an Illinois statute that prohibits state medical assistance payments for all abortions except those "necessary for the preservation of the life of the woman seeking such treatment." The [plaintiff, Williams was a physician] who perform[ed] medically necessary abortions for indigent women, a welfare rights organization, and Jane Doe, an indigent pregnant woman who alleged that she desired an abortion that was medically necessary, but not necessary to save her life. The defendant [Zbaraz] was the Director of the Illinois Department of Public Aid, the agency charged with administering the State's medical assistance programs. . . .

[Williams] challenged the Illinois statute on both federal statutory and constitutional grounds. [He] asserted, first, that Title XIX of the Social Security Act, commonly known as the "Medicaid" Act, requires Illinois to provide coverage in its Medicaid plan for all medically necessary abortions, whether or not the life of the pregnant woman is endangered. Second, [Williams] argued that the public funding by the State of medically necessary services generally, but not of certain medically necessary abortions, violates the Equal Protection Clause of the Fourteenth Amendment.

The District Court initially held that it would abstain from considering the complaint until the state courts had [interpreted] the challenged statute. [Williams] appealed,

and the Court of Appeals for the Seventh Circuit reversed. . . [and] remanded [returned] the case for further
proceedings. . . .

[T]he District Court concluded that Title XIX and the
regulations promulgated thereunder require a participating State under the Medicaid program to provide funding
for all medically necessary abortions. According to the
District Court, the so-called "Hyde Amendment" - under
which Congress has prohibited the use of federal funds to
reimburse the costs of certain medically necessary abortions - does not relieve a State of its independent obligation under Title XIX to provide Medicaid funding for all
medically necessary abortions. Thus, the District Court
permanently enjoined [stopped] the enforcement of the Illinois statute insofar as it denied payments for abortions
that are "medically necessary or medically indicated according to the professional medical judgment of a licensed
physician in Illinois, exercised in light of all factors affecting a woman's health."

The Court of Appeals again reversed. . . . [T]he court
held that the Hyde Amendment "alters Title XIX in such
a way as to allow states to limit funding to the categories
of abortions specified in that amendment." It further
held, however, that a participating State may not, consistent with Title XIX, withhold funding for those medically
necessary abortions for which federal reimbursement is
available under the Hyde Amendment. . . . The District
Court was specifically directed to consider "whether the
Hyde Amendment, by limiting funding for abortions to
certain circumstances even if such abortions are medically
necessary, violates the Fifth Amendment."

. . . [T]he District Court notified the Attorney General of the United States that the constitutionality of an Act of Congress had been drawn into question, and the United States intervened. . . to defend the Constitutionality of the Hyde Amendment. . . . [N]oting that the same reasoning would apply in determining the constitutional validity of both the Illinois statute and the Hyde Amendment, the District Court observed: "Although we are not persuaded that the federal and state enactments are inseparable and would hesitate to inject into the proceeding the issue of the constitutionality of a law not directly under attack by [Williams], we are obviously constrained to obey the Seventh Circuit's mandate. Therefore, while our discussion of the constitutional questions will address only the Illinois statute, the same analysis applies to the Hyde Amendment and the relief granted will encompass both laws."

The District Court then concluded that both the Illinois statute and the Hyde Amendment are unconstitutional insofar as they deny funding for "medically necessary abortions prior to the point of fetal viability." If the public funding of abortions were restricted to those covered by the Hyde Amendment, the District Court thought that the effect would "be to increase substantially maternal morbidity and mortality among indigent pregnant women." The District Court held that the state and federal funding restrictions violate the constitutional standard of equal protection because

"a pregnant woman's interest in her health so outweighs any possible state interest in the life of a nonviable fetus that, for a woman medically in need of an abortion, the state's interest is not legitimate. At the point of viability, however, 'the relative weights of the respective interests involved' shift, thereby legitimizing

the state's interests. After that point, therefore, . . . a
state may withhold funding for medically necessary
abortions that are not life-preserving, even though it
funds all other medically necessary operations."

Accordingly, the District Court enjoined [stopped] the Director of the Illinois Department of Public Aid from enforcing the Illinois statute to deny payment under the
state medical assistance programs for medically necessary
abortions prior to fetal viability. The District Court did
not, however, [stop] any action by the United States.

. . . . [T]he District Court was without jurisdiction to declare the Hyde Amendment unconstitutional, this Court
has jurisdiction over these appeals and thus may review
the "whole case."

. . . . Insofar as we have already concluded that the District Court lacked jurisdiction to declare the Hyde
Amendment unconstitutional, that portion of its judgment
must be vacated [annulled]. The remaining questions concern the Illinois statute. [Williams] argue[s] that (1) Title
XIX requires Illinois to provide coverage in its state Medicaid plan for all medically necessary abortions, whether
or not the life of the pregnant woman is endangered, and
(2) the funding by Illinois of medically necessary services
generally, but not of certain medically necessary abortions, violates the Equal Protection Clause of the Fourteenth Amendment. Both arguments are foreclosed by
our decision today in *Harris v. McRae*. . . . [W]e have
concluded in *McRae* that a participating State is not obligated under Title XIX to pay for those medically necessary abortions for which federal reimbursement is unavailable under the Hyde Amendment. As to [the] constitutional argument, we have concluded in *McRae* that the

Hyde Amendment does not violate the equal protection component of the Fifth Amendment by withholding public funding for certain medically necessary abortions, while providing funding for other medically necessary health services. It follows, for the same reasons, that the comparable funding restrictions in the Illinois statute do not violate the Equal Protection Clause of the Fourteenth Amendment.

Accordingly, the judgment of the District Court is [annulled], and the case is [returned] to that court for further proceedings consistent with this opinion.

It is so ordered.

JUSTICE BRENNAN (joined by Justices Marshall and Blackmun) dissented. [See the opinion in *Harris v. McRae*, p. 20.]

JUSTICE MARSHALL dissented. [See the opinion in *Harris v. McRae*, p. 24.]

JUSTICE BLACKMUN dissented. [See the opinion in *Harris v. McRae*, p. 30.]

JUSTICE STEVENS dissented. [See the opinion in *Harris v. McRae*, p. 30.]

H.L. v. MATHESON

EXCERPTS

"That the requirement of notice to parents may inhibit some minors from seeking abortions is not a valid basis to void the statute. . . . The Constitution does not compel a state to fine-tune its statutes so as to encourage or facilitate abortions."

Chief Justice Warren Burger

"In sum, a State may not validly require notice to parents in all cases, without providing an independent decision-maker to whom a pregnant minor can have recourse if she believes that she is mature enough to make the abortion decision independently or that notification otherwise would not be in her best interests. . . ."

Justice Lewis Powell

"Her choice, like the deeply intimate decisions to marry, to procreate, and to use contraceptives, is guarded from unwarranted state intervention by the right to privacy."

Justice Thurgood Marshall

In Brief

Question: Is Utah's parental notification statute constitutional?

Lower Court: Utah Supreme Court

Law: Utah Code, Section 76-7-304 (1974)

Parties: H.L., a pseudonym for a pregnant minor
Scott M. Matheson, Governor, Utah

Counsel: For H.L.: David Dolowitz
For Matheson: Paul Tinker

Arguments: October 6, 1980

Decision: March 23, 1981

Majority: Chief Justice Burger, Justices Stewart, White, Powell, Rehnquist, Stevens

Minority: Justices Brennan, Marshall, Blackmun

Decision by: Chief Justice Burger (p. 49)

Concurrences: Justice Powell (p. 55)
Justice Stevens (p. 58)

Dissents: Justice Marshall (p. 60)

Offical Text: U.S. Reports, Vol. 450, p. 398
Lower Court: Pacific Reporter 2d, Vol. 604, p. 907

THE H.L. COURT

Chief Justice Warren Burger
Appointed 1969 by Richard M. Nixon

Associate Justice William Brennan
Appointed 1956 by Dwight D. Eisenhower

Associate Justice Potter Stewart
Appointed 1958 by Dwight D. Eisenhower

Associate Justice Byron White
Appointed 1962 by John F. Kennedy

Associate Justice Thurgood Marshall
Appointed 1967 by Lyndon B. Johnson

Associate Justice Harry Blackmun
Appointed 1970 by Richard M. Nixon

Associate Justice Lewis Powell
Appointed 1972 by Richard M. Nixon

Associate Justice William Rehnquist
Appointed 1971 by Richard M. Nixon

Associate Justice John Paul Stevens
Appointed 1975 by Gerald R. Ford

H.L. v. MATHESON

March 23, 1981

CHIEF JUSTICE BURGER: The question presented in this case is whether a state statute which requires a physician to "notify, if possible," the parents of a dependent, unmarried minor girl prior to performing an abortion on the girl violates federal constitutional guarantees.

In the spring of 1978, appellant [H.L.] was an unmarried 15-year-old girl living with her parents in Utah and dependent on them for her support. She discovered she was pregnant. She consulted with a social worker and a physician. The physician advised [H.L.] that an abortion would be in her best medical interest. However, because of Utah [law], he refused to perform the abortion without first notifying [her] parents.

[The law], enacted in 1974, provides:

"To enable the physician to exercise his best medical judgment [in considering a possible abortion], he shall:

"(1) Consider all factors relevant to the well-being of the woman upon whom the abortion is to be performed including, but not limited to,

"(a) Her physical, emotional and psychological health and safety,

"(b) Her age,

"(c) Her familial situation.

"(2) *Notify, if possible, the parents or guardian of
the woman upon whom the abortion is to be performed, if she is a minor* or the husband of the
woman, if she is married."

Violation of this section is a misdemeanor punishable by
imprisonment for not more than one year or a fine of not
more than $1,000.

[H.L.] believed "for [her] own reasons" that she should
proceed with the abortion without notifying her parents.
According to [H.L.], the social worker concurred in this
decision. While still in the first trimester of her pregnancy, [H.L.] instituted this action in the Third Judicial District Court of Utah. She sought a declaration that [the
Utah law] is unconstitutional and an injunction [court order stopping an act] prohibiting appellees, the Governor
and the Attorney General of Utah, from enforcing the
statute. [H.L.] sought to represent a class [a group with
common characteristics] consisting of unmarried "minor
women who are suffering unwanted pregnancies and desire to terminate the pregnancies but may not do so" because of their physicians' insistence on complying with
[the law]. The trial judge declined to grant a temporary
restraining order or a preliminary injunction.

The trial judge held a hearing at which [H.L.] was the
only witness. [H.L.] affirmed [confirmed] the allegations
of the complaint by giving monosyllabic answers to her
attorney's leading questions. However, when the State attempted to cross-examine [H.L.] about her reasons for not
wishing to notify her parents, [H.L.]'s counsel vigorously
objected, insisting that "the specifics of the reasons are
really irrelevant to the Constitutional issue." The only
constitutionally permissible prerequisites for performance

of an abortion, he insisted, were the desire of the girl and the medical approval of a physician. The trial judge sustained [granted] the objection, tentatively construing [interpreting] the statute to require [H.L.]'s physician to notify her parents "if he is able to physically contact them."

. . . . On appeal, the Supreme Court of Utah unanimously upheld the statute. . . . [T]he court concluded that the statute serves "significant state interest[s]" that are present with respect to minors but absent in the case of adult women.

. . . . The Utah Supreme Court held that notifying the parents of a minor seeking an abortion is "substantially and logically related" to the *Doe* factors set out in Section 76-7-304(1) [of the Utah law] because parents ordinarily possess information essential to a physician's exercise of his best medical judgment concerning the child. The court also concluded that encouraging an unmarried pregnant minor to seek the advice of her parents in making the decision of whether to carry her child to term promotes a significant state interest in supporting the important role of parents in child-rearing. The court reasoned that since the statute allows no veto power over the minor's decision, it does not unduly intrude upon a minor's rights.

. . . . [H.L.] challenges the statute as unconstitutional. . . .

The trial court found that [H.L.] "is unmarried, fifteen years of age, resides at home and is a dependent of her parents." That affords an insufficient basis for a finding that she is either mature or emancipated. . . .

The only issue before us, then, is the ... constitutionality
of a statute requiring a physician to give notice to parents
"if possible," prior to performing an abortion on their
minor daughter, (a) when the girl is living with and dependent upon her parents, (b) when she is not emancipated by marriage or otherwise, and (c) when she has made
no claim or showing as to her maturity or as to her rela-
tions with her parents.

[H.L.] contends the statute violates the right to privacy
recognized in our prior cases with respect to abortions.
She places primary reliance on *Belotti II.* In *Danforth,* we
struck down state statutes that imposed a requirement of
prior written *consent* of the patient's spouse and of a min-
or patient's parents as a prerequisite for an abortion. ...

We emphasized, however, "that our holding ... does not
suggest that every minor, regardless of age or maturity,
may give effective consent for termination of her pregnancy." There is no logical relationship between the capacity to become pregnant and the capacity for mature
judgment concerning the wisdom of an abortion.

.... Although we have held that a state may not constitutionally legislate a blanket, unreviewable power of parents
to veto their daughter's abortion, a statute setting out a
"mere requirement of parental notice" does not violate the
constitutional rights of an immature, dependent minor.
Four Justices in *Belotti II* joined in stating:

".... [P]arental notice and consent are qualifications
that typically may be imposed by the State on a
minor's right to make important decisions. As immature minors often lack the ability to make fully informed choices that take account of both immediate

and long-range consequences, a State reasonably may determine that parental consultation often is desirable and in the best interest of the minor. It may further determine, as a general proposition, that such consultation is particularly desirable with respect to the abortion decision - one that for some people raises profound moral and religious concerns. . . ."

. . . . In addition, "constitutional interpretation has consistently recognized that the parents' claim to authority in their own household to direct the rearing of their children is basic in the structure of our society." . . .

We have recognized that parents have an important "guiding role" to play in the upbringing of their children, which presumptively includes counseling them on important decisions.

The Utah statute gives neither parents nor judges a veto power over the minor's abortion decision. As in *Belotti I*, "we are concerned with a statute directed toward minors, as to whom there are unquestionably greater risks of inability to give an informed consent." As applied to immature and dependent minors, the statute plainly serves the important considerations of family integrity and protecting adolescents which we identified in *Belotti II*. In addition . . . the statute serves a significant state interest by providing an opportunity for parents to supply essential medical and other information to a physician. The medical, emotional, and psychological consequences of an abortion are serious and can be lasting; this is particularly so when the patient is immature.   An adequate medical and psychological case history is important to the physician. . . .

[H.L.] intimates that the statute's failure to declare, in
terms, a detailed description of what information parents
may provide to physicians, or to provide for a mandatory
period of delay after the physician notifies the parents,
renders the statute unconstitutional. The notion that the
statute must itemize information to be supplied by parents finds no support in logic, experience, or our decisions.
And as the Utah Supreme Court recognized, time is likely
to be of the essence in an abortion decision. The Utah
statute is reasonably calculated to protect minors in
[H.L.]'s class [group with similar characteristics] by en-
hancing the potential for parental consultation concerning
a decision that has potentially traumatic and permanent
consequences.

[H.L.] also contends that the constitutionality of the statute is undermined because Utah allows a pregnant minor
to consent to other medical procedures without formal notice to her parents if she carries the child to term. But a
state's interests in full-term pregnancies are sufficiently
different to justify the line drawn by the statutes. If the
pregnant girl elects to carry her child to term, the *medical*
decisions to be made entail few - perhaps none - of the
potentially grave emotional and psychological consequences of the decision to abort.

That the requirement of notice to parents may inhibit
some minors from seeking abortions is not a valid basis to
void the statute . . . . The Constitution does not compel a
state to fine-tune its statutes so as to encourage or facilitate abortions. To the contrary, state action "encouraging
childbirth except in the most urgent circumstances" is
"rationally related to the legitimate governmental objective of protecting potential life."

.... [T]he statute plainly serves important state interests, is narrowly drawn to protect only those interests, and does not violate any guarantees of the Constitution. The judgment of the Supreme Court of Utah is affirmed.

JUSTICE POWELL (joined by Justice Stewart), concurring: This case requires the Court to consider again the divisive questions raised by a state statute intended to encourage parental involvement in the decision of a pregnant minor to have an abortion. I agree with the Court that [the Utah law] does not unconstitutionally burden [H.L.]'s right to an abortion. I join the opinion of the Court on the understanding that it leaves open the question whether [the Utah law] unconstitutionally burdens the right of a mature minor or a minor whose best interests would not be served by parental notification. ...

[H.L.] attacks this [parental] notice requirement on the ground that it burdens the right of a minor who is emancipated, or who is mature enough to make the abortion decision independently of parental involvement, or whose parents will react obstructively upon notice. ... The complaint in this case was carefully drawn. [H.L.]'s allegations about herself and her familial situation are few and laconic. She alleged that she did "not wish to inform her parents of her condition and believe[d] that it [was] in her best interest that her parents not be informed of her condition." She also alleged that she understood "what is involved in her decision," and that the physician she consulted had told her that "he could not and would not perform an abortion upon her without informing her parents prior to aborting her."

[H.L.] was 15 years of age and lived at home with her parents when she filed her complaint. She did not claim to be mature, and made no allegations with respect to her relationship with her parents. She did not aver that they would be obstructive if notified, or advance any other reason why notice to her parents would not be in her best interest. Similarly, the complaint contains no allegation that the physician - while apparently willing to perform the abortion - believed that notifying her parents would have adverse consequences. In fact, nothing in the record shows that the physician had any information about [H.L.]'s parents or familial situation, or even that he had examined [H.L.].

.... When [H.L.]'s lawyer insisted that the facts with respect to this particular minor were irrelevant, the trial court sustained [granted] the validity of the statute.

In sum, and as the Court's opinion emphasizes, [H.L.] alleges nothing more than that she desires an abortion, that she has decided - for reasons which she declined to reveal - that it is in her best interest not to notify her parents, and that a physician would be willing to perform the abortion if notice were not required. ... [T]hese bald allegations ... confer standing [the right] only to claim that [the Utah law] is an unconstitutional burden upon an unemancipated minor who desires an abortion without parental notification but also desires not to explain to anyone her reasons either for wanting the abortion or for not wanting to notify her parents.

.... I agree with the Court that [the Utah law] is not an unconstitutional burden on [H.L.]'s right to an abortion. Numerous and significant interests compete when a minor decides whether or not to abort her pregnancy. The right to make that decision may not be unconstitutionally burdened. In addition, the minor has an interest in effectuating her decision to abort, if that is the decision she makes. The State, aside from the interest it has in encouraging childbirth rather than abortion, has an interest in fostering such consultation as will assist the minor in making her decision as wisely as possible. The State also may have an interest in the family itself, the institution through which "we inculcate and pass down many of our most cherished values, moral and cultural." Parents have a traditional and substantial interest in, as well as a responsibility for, the rearing and welfare of their children, especially during immature years.

None of these interests is absolute. Even an adult woman's right to an abortion is not unqualified. Particularly when a minor becomes pregnant and considers an abortion, the relevant circumstances may vary widely depending upon her age, maturity, mental and physical condition, the stability of her home if she is not emancipated, her relationship with her parents, and the like. If we were to accept [H.L.]'s claim that [the Utah law] is per se an invalid burden on the asserted right of a minor to make the abortion decision, the circumstances which normally are relevant would - as her counsel insisted - be immaterial. The Court would have to decide that the minor's wishes are virtually absolute. To be sure, our cases have emphasized the necessity to consult a physician. But we have never held with respect to a minor that the opinion of a single physician as to the need or desirability of an abortion outweighs all state and parental interests.

In sum, a State may not validly require notice to parents in all cases, without providing an independent decision-maker to whom a pregnant minor can have recourse if she believes that she is mature enough to make the abortion decision independently or that notification otherwise would not be in her best interests. . . . The circumstances relevant to the abortion decision by a minor can and do vary so substantially that absolute rules - requiring parental notice in all cases or in none - would create an inflexibility that often would allow for no consideration of the rights and interests identified above. Our cases have never gone to this extreme, and in my view should not.

JUSTICE STEVENS, concurring: . . . . The Utah Supreme Court held that the [Utah Code] may validly be applied to all members of [the class of unmarried "'minor women who are suffering unwanted pregnancies and desire to terminate the pregnancies but may not do so' because of their physicians' insistence on complying with" . . . the Utah Code]. . . .

The fact that a state statute may have some impact upon a minor's exercise of his or her rights begins, rather than ends, the constitutional inquiry. Once the statute's impact is identified, it must be evaluated in light of the state interests underlying the statute. . . .

[T]he holding in *Roe v. Wade* that the abortion decision is entitled to constitutional protection merely emphasizes the importance of the decision; it does not lead to the conclusion that the state legislature has no power to enact legislation for the purpose of protecting a young pregnant woman from the consequences of an incorrect decision.

 . . . . In my opinion, the special importance of a young woman's abortion decision . . . provides a special justification for reasonable state efforts intended to ensure that the decision be wisely made. Such reasonable efforts surely may include a requirement that an abortion be procured only after consultation with a licensed physician.

And, because "the most significant consequences of the [abortion] decision are not medical in character," the State unquestionably has an interest in ensuring that a young woman receive other appropriate consultation as well. In my opinion, the quality of that interest is plainly sufficient to support a state legislature's determination that such appropriate consultation should include parental advice.

Of course, a conclusion that the Utah statute is invalid would not prevent young pregnant women from voluntarily seeking the advice of their parents prior to making the abortion decision. But the State may legitimately decide that such consultation should be made more probable by ensuring that parents are informed of their daughter's decision. . . .

Utah's interest in its parental-notice statute is not diminished by the fact that there can be no guarantee that meaningful parent-child consultation will actually occur. Good-faith compliance with the statute's requirements would tend to facilitate communication between daughters and parents regarding the abortion decision. The possibility that some parents will not react with compassion and understanding upon being informed of their daughter's predicament or that, even if they are receptive, they will incorrectly advise her, does not undercut the legitimacy of the State's attempt to establish a procedure that will enhance the probability that a pregnant young woman exercise as wisely as possible her right to make the abortion decision.

The fact that certain members of the class of unmarried "minor women who are suffering unwanted pregnancies and desire to terminate the pregnancies" may actually be emancipated or sufficiently mature to make a well-reasoned abortion decision does not, in my view, undercut the validity of the Utah statute. . . .

Because my view in this case, as in *Danforth*, is that the State's interest in protecting a young pregnant woman from the consequences of an incorrect abortion decision is sufficient to justify the parental-notice requirement, I agree that the decision of the Utah Supreme Court should be affirmed [confirmed].

JUSTICE MARSHALL (joined by Justices Brennan and Blackmun), dissenting: The decision of the Court is narrow. It finds shortcomings in [H.L.]'s complaint and therefore denies relief. . . .

Nonetheless, I dissent. I believe that even if the complaint is defective, the majority's legal analysis is incorrect and it yields an improper disposition here. More important, I cannot agree with the majority's view of the complaint, or its standing analysis. I therefore would reverse the judgment of the Supreme Court of Utah.

The Court finds [H.L.]'s complaint defective because it fails to allege that she is mature or emancipated, and neglects to specify her reasons for wishing to avoid notifying her parents about her abortion decision. . . .

[T]he Court does not question that [H.L.]'s injury due to the statute's requirement falls within the legally protected ambit of her privacy interest, and that the relief requested would remedy the harm. The Court decides only that [H.L.] cannot challenge the blanket nature of the statute because she neglected to allege that by her personal characteristics, she is a member of particular groups that undoubtedly deserve exemption from a parental notice requirement....

I am persuaded that [H.L.]'s complaint establishes a claim that notifying her parents would not be in her interests. She alleged that she "believes that it is in her best interest that her parents not be informed of her [pregnant] condition," and that after consulting with her physician, attorney, and social worker, "she understands what is involved in her decision" to seek an abortion.... In my judgment, [H.L.] has adequately asserted that she has persistently held reasons for believing parental notice would not be in her best interests. This provides a sufficient basis for standing [the right] to raise the challenge in her complaint. [H.L.] seeks to challenge a state statute, construed [interpreted] definitively by the highest court of that State to permit no exception to the notice requirement on the basis of any reasons offered by the minor....

[T]he trial court granted [H.L.]'s motion to represent a class, and it is undisputed that this class includes all "minor women who are suffering unwanted pregnancies and desire to terminate the pregnancies but may not do so inasmuch as their physicians will not perform an abortion upon them without compliance with the provisions of [the Utah law]." This class by definition includes all minor women, self-supporting or dependent, sophisticated or naive, as long as the Utah statute interferes with the ability of these women to decide with their physicians to obtain abortions.... [I]t is improper to assume [H.L.] adequately represents the entire class as defined by the trial court, but redefine the class [H.L.] is deemed to represent, and deny relief on that basis. Nonetheless, that is exactly the course selected by the majority today.

. . . . Our cases have established that a pregnant woman
has a fundamental right to choose whether to obtain an
abortion or carry the pregnancy to term. Her choice, like
the deeply intimate decisions to marry, to procreate, and
to use contraceptives, is guarded from unwarranted state
intervention by the right to privacy. Grounded in the
Due Process Clause of the Fourteenth Amendment, the
right to privacy protects both the woman's "interest in independence in making certain kinds of important decisions" and her "individual interest in avoiding disclosure
of personal matters."

In the abortion context, we have held that the right to
privacy shields the woman from undue state intrusion in,
and external scrutiny of, her very personal choice. Thus,
in *Roe v. Wade*, we held that during the first trimester of
the pregnancy, the State's interests in protecting maternal
health or the potential life of the fetus could not override
the right of the pregnant woman and the attending physician to make the abortion decision through private, unfettered consultation. We further emphasized the restricted
scope of permissible state action in this area when, in *Doe
v. Bolton*, we struck down state-imposed procedural requirements that subjected the woman's private decision
with her physician to review by other physicians and a
hospital committee.

It is also settled that the right to privacy, like many constitutional rights, extends to minors. Indeed, because an
unwanted pregnancy is probably more of a crisis for a
minor than for an adult, as the abortion decision cannot
be postponed until her majority, "there are few situations
in which denying a minor the right to make an important
decision will have consequences so grave and indelible."
Thus, for both the adult and the minor woman, state-

imposed burdens on the abortion decision can be justified only upon a showing that the restrictions advance "important state interests." Before examining the state interests asserted here, it is necessary first to consider Utah's claim that its statute does not "imping[e] on a woman's decision to have an abortion" or "plac[e] obstacles in the path of effectuating such a decision." This requires an examination of whether the parental notice requirement of the Utah statute imposes any burdens on the abortion decision.

The ideal of a supportive family so pervades our culture that it may seem incongruous to examine "burdens" imposed by a statute requiring parental notice of a minor daughter's decision to terminate her pregnancy. This Court has long deferred to the bonds which join family members for mutual sustenance. Especially in times of adversity, the relationships within a family can offer the security of constant caring and aid. Ideally, a minor facing an important decision will naturally seek advice and support from her parents, and they in turn will respond with comfort and wisdom. If the pregnant minor herself confides in her family, she plainly relinquishes her right to avoid telling or involving them. For a minor in that circumstance, the statutory requirement of parental notice hardly imposes a burden.

Realistically, however, many families do not conform to this ideal. Many minors, like [H.L.], oppose parental notice and seek instead to preserve the fundamental, personal right to privacy. It is for these minors that the parental notification requirement creates a problem. In this context, involving the minor's parents against her wishes effectively cancels her right to avoid disclosure of her personal choice. . . . Many minor women will encounter interference from their parents after the state-imposed notification. In addition to parental disappointment and disapproval, the minor may confront physical or emotional abuse, withdrawal of financial support, or actual obstruction of the abortion decision. Furthermore, the threat of parental notice may cause some minor women to delay past the first trimester of pregnancy, after which the health risks increase significantly. Other pregnant minors may attempt to self-abort or to obtain an illegal abortion rather than risk parental notification. Still others may foresake an abortion and bear an unwanted child, which, given the minor's "probable education, employment skills, financial resources and emotional maturity, . . . may be exceptionally burdensome." The possibility that such problems may not occur in particular cases does not alter the hardship created by the notice requirement on its face. And that hardship is not a mere disincentive created by the State, but is instead an actual state-imposed obstacle to the exercise of the minor woman's free choice. For the class of pregnant minors represented by [H.L.], this obstacle is so onerous as to bar the desired abortions. Significantly, the interference sanctioned by the statute does not operate in a neutral fashion. No notice is required for other pregnancy-related medical care, so only the minor women who wish to abort encounter the burden imposed by the notification statute. . . .

As established by this Court in *Planned Parenthood of Central Mo. v. Danforth*, the statute cannot survive [H.L.]'s challenge unless it is justified by a "significant state interest." Further, the State must demonstrate that the means it selected are closely tailored to serve that interest. . . .

In upholding the statute, the Utah Supreme Court concluded that the notification provision might encourage parental transmission of "additional information, which
might prove invaluable to the physician in exercising his
'best medical judgment.'" Yet neither the Utah courts nor
the statute itself specifies the kind of information contemplated for this purpose, nor why it is available to the
parents but not to the minor woman herself. Most parents lack the medical expertise necessary to supplement
the physician's medical judgment, and at best could provide facts about the patient's medical history. It seems
doubtful that a minor mature enough to become pregnant
and to seek medical advice on her own initiative would be
unable or unwilling to provide her physician with information crucial to the abortion decision. In addition, by
law the physician already is obligated to obtain all information necessary to form his best medical judgment, and
nothing bars consultation with the parents should the
physician find it necessary.

Even if mandatory parental notice serves a substantial
state purpose in this regard, the Utah statute fails to implement it.... Thus, the statute not only fails to promote
the transfer of information as is claimed, it does not apply
to other closely related contexts in which such exchange
of information would be no less important. The goal of
promoting consultation between the physician and the
parents of the pregnant minor cannot sustain a statute
that is so ill-fitted to serve it.

[Matheson] also claim[s] the statute serves the legitimate
purpose of improving the minor's decision by encouraging
consultation between the minor woman and her parents.
[Matheson] do[es] not dispute that the State cannot legally
or practically require such consultation.   Nor do[es

Matheson] contest the fact that the decision is ultimately the minor's to make. Nonetheless, the State seeks through the notice requirement to give parents the opportunity to contribute to the minor woman's abortion decision.

Ideally, facilitation of supportive conversation would assist the pregnant minor during an undoubtedly difficult experience. Again, however, when measured against the rationality of the means employed, the Utah statute simply fails to advance this asserted goal. The statute imposes no requirement that the notice be sufficiently timely to permit any discussion between the pregnant minor and the parents. . . . Parental consultation hardly seems a legitimate state purpose where the minor's pregnancy resulted from incest, where a hostile or abusive parental response is assured, or where the minor's fears of such a response deter her from the abortion she desires. The absolute nature of the statutory requirement, with exception permitted only if the parents are physically unavailable, violates the requirement that regulations in this fundamentally personal area be carefully tailored to serve a significant state interest. . . . I cannot approve [Utah's absolute notice requirement's] interference with the minor's private consultation with the physician during the first trimester of her pregnancy.

Finally, [Matheson] assert[s] a state interest in protecting parental authority and family integrity. This Court, of course, has recognized that the "primary role of the parents in the upbringing of their children is now established beyond debate as an enduring American tradition." Indeed, "those who nurture [the child] and direct his destiny have the right, coupled with the high duty, to recognize and prepare him for additional obligations." Similarly, our decisions "have respected the private realm of family life which the state cannot enter."

The critical thrust of these decisions has been to protect the privacy of individual families from unwarranted state intrusion. Ironically, [Matheson] invoke[s] these decisions in seeking to justify state interference in the normal functioning of the family. Through its notice requirement, the State in fact enters the private realm of the family rather than leaving unaltered the pattern of interactions chosen by the family. Whatever its motive, state intervention is hardly likely to resurrect parental authority that the parents themselves are unable to preserve. . . .

[W]hen the threat to parental authority originates not from the State but from the minor child, invocation of "reserved" rights of parents cannot sustain [grant] blanket state intrusion into family life such as that mandated by the Utah statute. Such a result not only runs counter to the private domain of the family which the State may not breach; it also conflicts with the limits traditionally placed on parental authority. Parental authority is never absolute, and has been denied legal protection when its exercise threatens the health or safety of the minor children. Indeed, legal protection for parental rights is frequently tempered if not replaced by concern for the child's interest. Whatever its importance elsewhere, parental authority deserves . . . legal reinforcement where the minor's exercise of a fundamental right is burdened.

To decide this case, there is no need to determine whether parental rights never deserve legal protection when their assertion conflicts with the minor's rights and interests. I conclude that this statute cannot be defended as a mere reinforcement of existing parental rights, for the statute reaches beyond the legal limits of those rights. The statute applies, without exception, to emancipated minors, mature minors, and minors with emergency health care needs, all of whom, as Utah recognizes, by law have long been entitled to medical care unencumbered by parental involvement. . . . Utah's rejection of any exception to the notice requirement for a pregnant minor is plainly overbroad. In *Belotti II*, we were unwilling to cut a pregnant minor off from any avenue to obtain help beyond her parents, and yet the Utah statute does just that.

In this area, I believe this Court must join the state courts and legislatures which have acknowledged the undoubted social reality: some minors, in some circumstances, have the capacity and need to determine their health care needs without involving their parents. . . . Utah itself has allocated pregnancy-related health care decisions entirely to the pregnant minor. Where the physician has cause to doubt the minor's actual ability to understand and consent, by law he must pursue the requisites of the State's informed consent procedures. The State cannot have a legitimate interest in adding to this scheme mandatory parental notice of the minor's abortion decision. This conclusion does not affect parents' traditional responsibility to guide their children's development, especially in personal and moral concerns. I am persuaded that the Utah notice requirement is not necessary to assure parents this traditional child-rearing role, and that it burdens the minor's fundamental right to choose with her physician whether to terminate her pregnancy.

. . . . Rather than serving to enhance the physician's judgment, in cases such as [H.L.]'s, the statute prevents implementation of the physician's medical recommendation. Rather than promoting the transfer of information held by parents to the minor's physician, the statute neglects to require anything more than a communication from the physician moments before the abortion. Rather than respecting the private realm of family life, the statute invokes the criminal machinery of the State in an attempt to influence the interactions within the family. Accordingly, I would reverse the judgment of the Supreme Court of Utah insofar as it upheld the statute against constitutional attack.

AKRON v. AKRON CENTER

EXCERPTS

"The Court has also recognized, because abortion is a medical procedure, that the full vindication of the woman's fundamental right necessarily requires that her physician be given 'the room he needs to make his best medical judgment.' The physician's exercise of this medical judgment encompasses both assisting the woman in the decisionmaking process and implementing her decision should she choose abortion."

Justice Lewis Powell

"'*Roe* did not declare an unqualified "constitutional right to an abortion."' Rather, the *Roe* right is intended to protect against state action 'drastically limiting the availability and safety of the desired service' against the imposition of an 'absolute obstacle' on the abortion decision, or against 'official interference' and 'coercive restraint' imposed on the abortion decision. That a state regulation may 'inhibit' abortions to some degree does not require that we find that the regulation is invalid."

Justice Sandra Day O'Connor

In Brief

Question: Is the abortion ordinance of Akron, Ohio constitutional?

Lower Court: U.S. District Court, Northern Ohio
U.S. Court of Appeals, Sixth Circuit

Law: Akron Ordinance No. 160-1978, entitled "Regulation of Abortions"

Parties: City of Akron
Akron Center for Reproductive Health

Counsel: For Akron: Alan Segedy
For Akron Center: Stephan Landsman

Arguments: November 30, 1982

Decision: June 15, 1983

Majority: Chief Justice Burger, Justices Brennan, Marshall, Blackmun, Powell, Stevens

Minority: Justices White, Rehnquist, O'Connor

Decision by: Justice Powell (p. 75)

Dissents: Justice O'Connor (p. 91)

Offical Text: U.S. Reports, Vol. 462, p. 416
Lower Court: Federal Supplement, Vol. 479, p. 1172
Federal Reporter 2d, Vol. 651, p. 1198

THE AKRON COURT

Chief Justice Warren Burger
Appointed 1969 by Richard M. Nixon

Associate Justice William Brennan
Appointed 1956 by Dwight D. Eisenhower

Associate Justice Byron White
Appointed 1962 by John F. Kennedy

Associate Justice Thurgood Marshall
Appointed 1967 by Lyndon B. Johnson

Associate Justice Harry Blackmun
Appointed 1970 by Richard M. Nixon

Associate Justice Lewis Powell
Appointed 1972 by Richard M. Nixon

Associate Justice William Rehnquist
Appointed 1971 by Richard M. Nixon

Associate Justice John Paul Stevens
Appointed 1975 by Gerald R. Ford

Associate Justice Sandra Day O'Connor
Appointed 1981 by Ronald W. Reagan

AKRON v. AKRON CENTER

June 15, 1983

JUSTICE POWELL: In this litigation we must decide the constitutionality of several provisions of an ordinance enacted by the city of Akron, Ohio, to regulate the performance of abortions. Today we also review abortion regulations enacted by the State of Missouri [Planned Parenthood Association of Kansas City, Missouri, Inc. v. Ashcroft] and by the State of Virginia [Simopoulos v. Virginia].

These cases come to us a decade after we held in *Roe v. Wade* that the right of privacy, grounded in the concept of personal liberty guaranteed by the Constitution, encompasses a woman's right to decide whether to terminate her pregnancy. Legislative responses to the Court's decision have required us on several occasions, and again today, to define the limits of a State's authority to regulate the performance of abortions. And arguments continue to be made, in these cases as well, that we erred in interpreting the Constitution. Nonetheless, the doctrine of stare decisis [let past decisions stand], while perhaps never entirely persuasive on a constitutional question, is a doctrine that demands respect in a society governed by the rule of law. We respect it today, and reaffirm *Roe v. Wade*.

In February 1978 the City Council of Akron enacted Ordinance No. 160-1978, entitled "Regulation of Abortions." The ordinance sets forth 17 provisions that regulate the performance of abortions, 5 of which are at issue in this case:

(i) Section 1870.03 requires that all abortions performed after the first trimester of pregnancy be performed in a hospital.

(ii) Section 1870.05 sets forth requirements for notification of and consent by parents before abortions may be performed on unmarried minors.

(iii) Section 1870.06 requires that the attending physician make certain specified statements to the patient "to insure that the consent for an abortion is truly informed consent."

(iv) Section 1870.07 requires a 24-hour waiting period between the time the woman signs a consent form and the time the abortion is performed.

(v) Section 1870.16 requires that fetal remains be "disposed of in a humane and sanitary manner."

A violation of any section of the ordinance is punishable as a criminal misdemeanor. If any provision is invalidated, it is to be severed from the remainder of the ordinance. The ordinance became effective on May 1, 1978.

On April 19, 1978, a lawsuit challenging virtually all of the ordinance's provisions was filed in the District Court for the Northern District of Ohio. The plaintiffs . . . were three corporations that operate abortion clinics in *Akron* and a physician who has performed abortions at one of the clinics. The defendants . . . were the city of Akron and three city officials. . . . Two individuals . . . were permitted to intervene as codefendants "in their individual capacity as parents of unmarried minor daughters of childbearing age." On April 27, 1978, the District Court preliminarily enjoined [stopped] enforcement of the ordinance.

In August 1979, after hearing evidence, the District Court ... invalidated four provisions, including Section 1870.05 (parental notice and consent), Section 1870.06(B) (requiring disclosure of facts concerning the woman's pregnancy, fetal development, the complications of abortion, and agencies available to assist the woman), and Section 1870.16 (disposal of fetal remains). The court upheld the constitutionality of the remainder of the ordinance, including Section 1870.03 (hospitalization for abortions after the first trimester), Section 1870.06(C) (requiring disclosure of the particular risks of the woman's pregnancy and the abortion technique to be employed), and Section 1870.07 (24-hour waiting period).

All parties appealed some portion of the District Court's judgment. The Court of Appeals for the Sixth Circuit ... affirmed the District Court's decision that Section 1870.03's hospitalization requirement is constitutional. It also affirmed the ruling that Sections 1870.05, 1870.06(B), and 1870.16 are unconstitutional. The Court of Appeals reversed the District Court's decision on Sections 1870.06(C) and 1870.07, finding these provisions to be unconstitutional.

.... In light of the importance of the issues presented, and in particular the conflicting decisions as to whether a State may require that all second-trimester abortions be performed in a hospital, we granted both Akron's and [Akron Center's] petitions. ... We now reverse the judgment of the Court of Appeals upholding Akron's hospitalization requirement, but affirm [confirm] the remainder of the decision invalidating the provisions on parental

consent, informed consent, waiting period, and disposal of
fetal remains.

In *Roe v. Wade*, the Court held that the "right of privacy,
. . . founded in the Fourteenth Amendment's concept of
personal liberty and restrictions upon state action, . . . is
broad enough to encompass a woman's decision whether
or not to terminate her pregnancy." Although the Constitution does not specifically identify this right, the history
of this Court's constitutional adjudication leaves no doubt
that "the full scope of the liberty guaranteed by the Due
Process Clause cannot be found in or limited by the precise terms of the specific guarantees elsewhere provided
in the Constitution." Central among these protected liberties is an individual's "freedom of personal choice in matters of marriage and family life." The decision in *Roe*
was based firmly on this long-recognized and essential element of personal liberty.

The Court also has recognized, because abortion is a medical procedure, that the full vindication of the woman's
fundamental right necessarily requires that her physician
be given "the room he needs to make his best medical
judgment." The physician's exercise of this medical judgment encompasses both assisting the woman in the decisionmaking process and implementing her decision should
she choose abortion.

At the same time, the Court in *Roe* acknowledged that the
woman's fundamental right "is not unqualified and must
be considered against important state interests in
abortion." But restrictive state regulation of the right to
choose abortion, as with other fundamental rights subject
to searching judicial examination, must be supported by a

compelling state interest. We have recognized two such interests that may justify state regulation of abortions.

First, a State has an "important and legitimate interest in protecting the potentiality of human life." Although the interest exists "throughout the course of the woman's pregnancy," it becomes compelling only at viability, the point at which the fetus "has the capability of meaningful life outside the mother's womb." At viability this interest in protecting the potential life of the unborn child is so important that the State may proscribe abortions altogether, "except when it is necessary to preserve the life or health of the mother."

Second, because a State has a legitimate concern with the health of women who undergo abortions, "a State may properly assert important interests in safeguarding health [and] in maintaining medical standards." We held in *Roe*, however, that this health interest does not become compelling until "approximately the end of the first trimester" of pregnancy. Until that time, a pregnant woman must be permitted, in consultation with her physician, to decide to have an abortion and to effectuate that decision "free of interference by the State."

This does not mean that a State never may enact a regulation touching on the woman's abortion right during the first weeks of pregnancy. Certain regulations that have no significant impact on the woman's exercise of her right may be permissible where justified by important state health objectives. . . . But even these minor regulations on the abortion procedure during the first trimester may not interfere with physician-patient consultation or with the woman's choice between abortion and childbirth.

From approximately the end of the first trimester of
pregnancy, the State "may regulate the abortion procedure
to the extent that the regulation reasonably relates to the
preservation and protection of maternal health." The
State's discretion to regulate on this basis does not, however, permit it to adopt abortion regulations that depart
from accepted medical practice. . . . If a State requires licensing or undertakes to regulate the performance of
abortions during this period, the health standards adopted
must be "legitimately related to the objective the State
seeks to accomplish."

Section 1870.03 of the Akron ordinance requires that any
abortion performed "upon a pregnant woman subsequent
to the end of the first trimester of her pregnancy" must
be "performed in a hospital." A "hospital" is "a general
hospital or special hospital devoted to gynecology or obstetrics which is accredited by the Joint Commission on
Accreditation of Hospitals or by the American Osteopathic Association." Accreditation by these organizations requires compliance with comprehensive standards governing a wide variety of health and surgical services. The ordinance thus prevents the performance of abortions in
outpatient facilities that are not part of an acute-care,
full-service hospital.

In the District Court [Akron Center] sought to demonstrate that this hospitalization requirement has a serious
detrimental impact on a woman's ability to obtain a second-trimester abortion in Akron and that it is not reasonably related to the State's interest in the health of the
pregnant woman. The District Court did not reject this
argument, but rather found the evidence "not . . . so convincing that it is willing to discard the Supreme Court's
formulation in *Roe*" of a line between impermissible

first-trimester regulation and permissible second-trimester regulation. The Court of Appeals affirmed on a similar basis. It accepted [Akron Center's] argument that Akron's hospitalization requirement did not have a reasonable health justification during at least part of the second trimester, but declined to "retreat from the 'bright line' in *Roe v. Wade.*" We believe that the courts below misinterpreted this Court's prior decisions, and we now hold that Section 1870.03 is unconstitutional.

In *Roe v. Wade* the Court held that after the end of the first trimester of pregnancy the State's interest becomes compelling, and it may "regulate the abortion procedure to the extent that the regulation reasonably relates to the preservation and protection of maternal health." ...

We reaffirm today that a State's interest in health regulation becomes compelling at approximately the end of the first trimester. The existence of a compelling state interest in health, however, is only the beginning of the inquiry. The State's regulation may be upheld only if it is reasonably designed to further that state interest. And the Court in *Roe* did not hold that it always is reasonable for a State to adopt an abortion regulation that applies to the entire second trimester. ... [T]he State is obligated to make a reasonable effort to limit the effect of its regulations to the period in the trimester during which its health interest will be furthered.

There can be no doubt that Section 1870.03's second-trimester hospitalization requirement places a significant obstacle in the path of women seeking an abortion. A primary burden created by the requirement is additional cost to the woman. ... [A] second-trimester hospitalization requirement may force women to travel to find available facilities, resulting in both financial expense and additional health risk. It therefore is apparent that a second-trimester hospitalization requirement may significantly limit a woman's ability to obtain an abortion.

Akron does not contend that Section 1870.03 imposes only an insignificant burden on women's access to abortion, but rather defends it as a reasonable health regulation. This position had strong support at the time of *Roe v. Wade*, as hospitalization for second-trimester abortions was recommended by the American Public Health Association (APHA) and the American College of Obstetricians and Gynecologists (ACOG). Since then, however, the safety of second-trimester abortions has increased dramatically. The principal reason is that the D&E [dilation & evacuation] procedure is now widely and successfully used for second-trimester abortions. The Court of Appeals found that there was "an abundance of evidence that D&E is the safest method of performing post-first trimester abortions today." The availability of the D&E procedure during the interval between approximately 12 and 16 weeks of pregnancy, a period during which other second-trimester abortion techniques generally cannot be used, has meant that women desiring an early second-trimester abortion no longer are forced to incur the health risks of waiting until at least the 16th week of pregnancy.

For our purposes, an even more significant factor is that experience indicates that D&E may be performed safely on an outpatient basis in appropriate nonhospital facilities. The evidence is strong enough to have convinced the APHA to abandon its prior recommendation of hospitalization for all second-trimester abortions. . . . Similarly, the ACOG no longer suggests that all second-trimester abortions be performed in a hospital. It recommends that abortions performed in a physician's office or outpatient clinic be limited to 14 weeks of pregnancy, but it indicates that abortions may be performed safely in "a hospital-based or in a free-standing ambulatory surgical facility, or in an out-patient clinic meeting the criteria required for a free-standing surgical facility," until 18 weeks of pregnancy.

These developments, and the professional commentary supporting them, constitute impressive evidence that - at least during the early weeks of the second trimester - D&E abortions may be performed as safely in an outpatient clinic as in a full-service hospital. We conclude, therefore, that "present medical knowledge" convincingly undercuts Akron's justification for requiring that *all* second-trimester abortions be performed in a hospital.

Akron nonetheless urges that "[t]he fact that some midtrimester abortions may be done in a minimally equipped clinic does not invalidate the regulation." It is true that a state abortion regulation is not unconstitutional simply because it does not correspond perfectly in all cases to the asserted state interest. But the lines drawn in a state regulation must be reasonable, and this cannot be said of Section 1870.03. . . . Section 1870.03 has "the effect of inhibiting . . . the vast majority of abortions after the first 12 weeks," and therefore unreasonably infringes upon a woman's constitutional right to obtain an abortion.

We turn next to Section 1870.05(B), the provision prohibiting a physician from performing an abortion on a minor pregnant woman under the age of 15 unless he obtains "the informed written consent of one of her parents or her legal guardian" or unless the minor obtains "an order from a court having jurisdiction over her that the abortion be performed or induced." ...

The relevant legal standards are not in dispute. The Court has held that "the State may not impose a blanket provision . . . requiring the consent of a parent or person in loco parentis [in place of the parent] as a condition for abortion of an unmarried minor." In *Belotti v. Baird* (*Belotti II*), a majority of the Court indicated that a State's interest in protecting immature minors will sustain a requirement of a consent substitute, either parental or judicial. The *Belotti II* plurality cautioned, however, that the State must provide an alternative procedure whereby a pregnant minor may demonstrate that she is sufficiently mature to make the abortion decision herself or that, despite her immaturity, an abortion would be in her best interests. Under these decisions, it is clear that Akron may not make a blanket determination that *all* minors under the age of 15 are too immature to make this decision or that an abortion never may be in the minor's best interests without parental approval.

Akron's ordinance does not create expressly the alternative procedure required by *Belotti II*. ...

[W]e do not think that the Akron ordinance, as applied in Ohio juvenile proceedings, is reasonably susceptible of being construed [interpreted] to create an "opportunity for case-by-case evaluations of the maturity of pregnant minors." We therefore affirm the Court of Appeals' judgment that Section 1870.05(B) is unconstitutional.

The Akron ordinance provides that no abortion shall be performed except "with the informed written consent of the pregnant woman, . . . given freely and without coercion." Furthermore, "in order to insure that the consent for an abortion is truly informed consent," the woman must be "orally informed by her attending physician" of the status of her pregnancy, the development of her fetus, the date of possible viability, the physical and emotional complications that may result from an abortion, and the availability of agencies to provide her with assistance and information with respect to birth control, adoption, and childbirth. In addition, the attending physician must inform her "of the particular risks associated with her own pregnancy and the abortion technique to be employed . . . [and] other information which in his own medical judgment is relevant to her decision as to whether to have an abortion or carry her pregnancy to term."

The District Court found that Section 1870.06(B) was unconstitutional, but that Section 1870.06(C) was related to a valid state interest in maternal health. The Court of Appeals concluded that both provisions were unconstitutional. We affirm.

In *Danforth*, we upheld a Missouri law requiring a pregnant woman to "certif[y] in writing her consent to the abortion and that her consent is informed and freely given and is not the result of coercion." . . .

We rejected the view that "informed consent" was too vague a term, construing [interpreting] it to mean "the giving of information to the patient as to just what would be done and as to its consequences. To ascribe more meaning than this might well confine the attending physician in an undesired and uncomfortable straitjacket in the practice of his profession."

The validity of an informed consent requirement thus rests on the State's interest in protecting the health of the pregnant woman. The decision to have an abortion has "implications far broader than those associated with most other kinds of medical treatment," and thus the State legitimately may seek to ensure that it has been made "in the light of all attendant circumstances - psychological and emotional as well as physical - that might be relevant to the well-being of the patient." This does not mean, however, that a State has unreviewable authority to decide what information a woman must be given before she chooses to have an abortion. It remains primarily the responsibility of the physician to ensure that appropriate information is conveyed to his patient, depending on her particular circumstances. *Danforth's* recognition of the State's interest in ensuring that this information be given will not justify abortion regulations designed to influence the woman's informed choice between abortion or childbirth.

Viewing the city's regulations in this light, we believe that Section 1870.06(B) attempts to extend the State's interest in ensuring "informed consent" beyond permissible limits. . . . Subsection (3) requires the physician to inform his patient that "the unborn child is a human life from the moment of conception," a requirement inconsistent with the Court's holding in *Roe v. Wade* that a State may not adopt one theory of when life begins to justify its regulation of abortions. Moreover, much of the detailed description of "the anatomical and physiological characteristics of the particular unborn child" required by subsection (3) would involve at best speculation by the physician. And subsection (5), that begins with the dubious statement that "abortion is a major surgical procedure" and proceeds to describe numerous possible physical and psychological complications of abortion, is a "parade of horribles" intended to suggest that abortion is a particularly dangerous procedure.

An additional, and equally decisive, objection to Section 1870.06(B) is its intrusion upon the discretion of the pregnant woman's physician. This provision specifies a litany of information that the physician must recite to each woman regardless of whether in his judgment the information is relevant to her personal decision. . . . In *Danforth* the Court warned against placing the physician in just such an "undesired and uncomfortable straitjacket." Consistent with its interest in ensuring informed consent, a State may require that a physician make certain that his patient understands the physical and emotional implications of having an abortion. But Akron has gone far beyond merely describing the general subject matter relevant to informed consent. By insisting upon recitation of a lengthy and inflexible list of information, Akron unreasonably has placed "obstacles in the path of the doctor upon whom [the woman is] entitled to rely for advice in connection with her decision."

Section 1870.06(C) presents a different question. Under this provision, the "attending physician" must inform the woman

"of the particular risks associated with her own pregnancy and the abortion technique to be employed including providing her with at least a general description of the medical instructions to be followed subsequent to the abortion in order to insure her safe recovery, and shall in addition provide her with such other information which in his own medical judgment is relevant to her decision as to whether to have an abortion vant to her decision as to whether to have an abortion or carry her pregnancy to term."

The information required clearly is related to maternal health and to the State's legitimate purpose in requiring informed consent. Nonetheless, the Court of Appeals determined that it interfered with the physician's medical judgment "in exactly the same way as section 1870.06(B). . . . We see no significant difference in Akron's requirement that the woman be told of the particular risks of her pregnancy and the abortion technique to be used, and be given general instructions on proper post abortion care. . . . Section 1870.06(C) merely describes in general terms the information to be disclosed. It properly leaves the precise nature and amount of this disclosure to the physician's discretion and "medical judgment."

. . . . Requiring physicians personally to discuss the abortion decision, its health risks, and consequences with each patient may in some cases add to the cost of providing abortions, though the record here does not suggest that ethical physicians will charge more for adhering to this typical element of the physician-patient relationship. Yet in *Roe* and subsequent cases we have "stressed repeatedly the central role of the physician, both in consulting with the woman about whether or not to have an abortion, and in determining how any abortion was to be carried out." Moreover, we have left no doubt that, to ensure the safety of the abortion procedure, the States may mandate that only physicians perform abortions.

We are not convinced, however, that there is as vital a state need for insisting that the physician performing the abortion, or for that matter any physician, personally counsel the patient in the absence of a request. The

State's interest is in ensuring that the woman's consent is informed and unpressured; the critical factor is whether she obtains the necessary information and counseling from a qualified person, not the identity of the person from whom she obtains it. . . . [W]e cannot say that the woman's consent to the abortion will not be informed if a physician delegates the counseling task to another qualified individual.

In so holding, we do not suggest that the State is powerless to vindicate its interest in making certain the "important" and "stressful" decision to abort "[is] made with full knowledge of its nature and consequences." Nor do we imply that a physician may abdicate his essential role as the person ultimately responsible for the medical aspects of the decision to perform the abortion. A State may define the physician's responsibility to include verification that adequate counseling has been provided and that the woman's consent is informed. In addition, the State may establish reasonable minimum qualifications for those people who perform the primary counseling function. In light of these alternatives, we believe that it is unreasonable for a State to insist that only a physician is competent to provide the information and counseling relevant to informed consent. We affirm the judgment of the Court of Appeals that Section 1870.06(C) is invalid.

The Akron ordinance prohibits a physician from performing an abortion until 24 hours after the pregnant woman signs a consent form. The District Court upheld this provision on the ground that it furthered Akron's interest in ensuring "that a woman's abortion decision is made after careful consideration of all the facts applicable to her particular situation." The Court of Appeals reversed, finding that the inflexible waiting period had "no medical basis," and that careful consideration of the abortion decision by the woman "is beyond the state's power to require." We affirm the Court of Appeals' judgment.

. . . . We find that Akron has failed to demonstrate that any legitimate state interest is furthered by an arbitrary and inflexible waiting period. There is no evidence suggesting that the abortion procedure will be performed more safely. Nor are we convinced that the State's legitimate concern that the woman's decision be informed is reasonably served by requiring a 24-hour delay as a matter of course. The decision whether to proceed with an abortion is one as to which it is important to "affor[d] the physician adequate discretion in the exercise of his medical judgment." In accordance with the ethical standards of the profession, a physician will advise the patient to defer the abortion when he thinks this will be beneficial to her. But if a woman, after appropriate counseling, is prepared to give her written informed consent and proceed with the abortion, a State may not demand that she delay the effectuation of that decision.

Section 1870.16 of the Akron ordinance requires physicians performing abortions to "insure that the remains of the unborn child are disposed of in a humane and sanitary manner." The Court of Appeals . . . invalidated the entire provision, declining to sever the word "humane" in order to uphold the requirement that disposal be "sanitary." We affirm this judgment.

. . . . Because Section 1870.16 fails to give a physician "fair notice that his contemplated conduct is forbidden," we agree that it violates the Due Process Clause.

We affirm the judgment of the Court of Appeals invalidating those sections of Akron's "Regulations of Abortions" ordinance that deal with parental consent, informed consent, a 24-hour waiting period, and the disposal of fetal remains. The remaining portion of the judgment, sustaining [granting] Akron's requirement that all second-trimester abortions be performed in a hospital, is reversed.

It is so ordered.

JUSTICE O'CONNOR (joined by Justices White and Rehnquist), dissenting: In *Roe v. Wade*, the Court held that the "right of privacy . . . founded in the Fourteenth Amendment's concept of personal liberty and restrictions upon state action . . . is broad enough to encompass a woman's decision whether or not to terminate her pregnancy." The parties in these cases have not asked the Court to re-examine the validity of that holding and the court below did not address it. Accordingly, the Court does not re-examine its previous holding. Nonetheless, it is apparent from the Court's opinion that neither sound constitutional theory nor our need to decide cases based on the application of neutral principles can accommodate an analytical framework that varies according to the "stages" of pregnancy, where those stages, and their concomitant standards of review, differ according to the level of medical technology available when a particular challenge to state regulation occurs. The Court's analysis of the Akron regulations is inconsistent both with the methods of analysis employed in previous cases dealing with abortion, and with the Court's approach to fundamental rights in other areas.

Our recent cases indicate that a regulation imposed on "a lawful abortion 'is not unconstitutional unless it unduly

burdens the right to seek an abortion.'" In my view, this
"unduly burdensome" standard should be applied to the
challenged regulations throughout the entire pregnancy
without reference to the particular "stage" of pregnancy
involved. If the particular regulation does not "unduly
burde[n]" the fundamental right, then our evaluation of
that regulation is limited to our determination that the
regulation rationally relates to a legitimate state purpose.
Irrespective of what we may believe is wise or prudent
policy in this difficult area, "the Constitution does not
constitute us as 'Platonic Guardians' nor does it vest in
this Court the authority to strike down laws because they
do not meet our standards of desirable social policy,
'wisdom,' or 'common sense.'"

The trimester or "three-stage" approach adopted by the
Court in *Roe*, and, in a modified form, employed by the
Court to analyze the regulations in these cases, cannot be
supported as a legitimate or useful framework for accommodating the woman's right and the State's interests. The
decision of the Court today graphically illustrates why the
trimester approach is a completely unworkable method of
accommodating the conflicting personal rights and compelling state interests that are involved in the abortion
context.

As the Court indicates today, the State's compelling interest in maternal health changes as medical technology
changes, and any health regulation must not "depart from
accepted medical practice." In applying this standard, the
Court holds that "the safety of second-trimester abortions
has increased dramatically" since 1973, when *Roe* was decided. Although a regulation such as one requiring that
all second-trimester abortions be performed in hospitals
"had strong support" in 1973 "as a reasonable health regu-

lation," this regulation can no longer stand because, according to the Court's diligent research into medical and scientific literature, the dilation and evacuation procedure (D&E), used in 1973 only for first-trimester abortions, "is now widely and successfully used for second-trimester abortions." Further, the medical literature relied on by the Court indicates that the D&E procedure may be performed in an appropriate nonhospital setting for "at least . . . the early weeks of the second trimester. . . ." The Court then chooses the period of 16 weeks of gestation as that point at which D&E procedures may be performed safely in a nonhospital setting, and thereby invalidates the Akron hospitalization regulation.

It is not difficult to see that despite the Court's purported adherence to the trimester approach adopted in *Roe*, the lines drawn in that decision have now been "blurred" because of what the Court accepts as technological advancement in the safety of abortion procedure. The State may no longer rely on a "bright line" that separates permissible from impermissible regulation, and it is no longer free to consider the second trimester as a unit and weigh the risks posed by all abortion procedures throughout that trimester. Rather, the State must continuously and conscientiously study contemporary medical and scientific literature in order to determine whether the effect of a particular regulation is to "depart from accepted medical practice" insofar as particular procedures and particular periods within the trimester are concerned. Assuming that legislative bodies are able to engage in this exacting task, it is difficult to believe that our Constitution *requires* that they do it as a prelude to protecting the health of their citizens. It is even more difficult to believe that this Court, without the resources available to those bodies entrusted with making legislative choices, believes itself competent to make these inquiries and to revise these standards every time the American College of Obstetricians and Gynecologists (ACOG) or similar group revises its views about what is and what is not appropriate medical procedure in this area. Indeed, the ACOG Standards on which the Court relies were changed in 1982 after trial in the present cases. Before ACOG changed its Standards in 1982, it recommended that all mid-trimester abortions be performed in a hospital. As today's decision indicates, medical technology is changing, and this change will necessitate our continued functioning as the Nation's "ex officio medical board with powers to approve or disapprove medical and operative practices and standards throughout the United States."

Just as improvements in medical technology inevitably will move *forward* the point at which the State may regulate for reasons of maternal health, different technological improvements will move *backward* the point of viability at which the State may proscribe abortions except when necessary to preserve the life and health of the mother.

In 1973, viability before 28 weeks was considered unusual. The 14th edition of L. Hellman & J. Pritchard, *Williams Obstetrics*, on which the Court relied in *Roe* for its understanding of viability, stated that "[a]ttainment of a [fetal] weight of 1,000 g [or a fetal age of approximately 28 weeks gestation] is . . . widely used as the criterion of viability." However, recent studies have demonstrated increasingly earlier fetal viability. It is certainly reasonable to believe that fetal viability in the first trimester of pregnancy may be possible in the not too distant future. Indeed, the Court has explicitly acknowledged that *Roe* left the point of viability "flexible for anticipated advancements in medical skill." "[W]e recognized in *Roe* that viability was a matter of medical judgment, skill, and technical ability, and we preserved the flexibility of the term."

The *Roe* framework, then, is clearly on a collision course with itself. As the medical risks of various abortion procedures decrease, the point at which the State may regulate for reasons of maternal health is moved further forward to actual childbirth. As medical science becomes better able to provide for the separate existence of the fetus, the point of viability is moved further back toward conception. Moreover, it is clear that the trimester approach violates the fundamental aspiration of judicial decisionmaking through the application of neutral principles "sufficiently absolute to give them roots throughout the community and continuity over significant periods of time. . . ." The *Roe* framework is inherently tied to the state of medical technology that exists whenever particular litigation ensues. Although legislatures are better suited to make the necessary factual judgments in this area, the Court's framework forces legislatures, as a matter of constitutional law, to speculate about what constitutes "accepted medical practice" at any given time. Without the necessary expertise or ability, courts must then pretend to act as science review boards and examine those legislative judgments.

The Court adheres to the *Roe* framework because the doctrine of stare decisis [let past decisions stand] "demands respect in a society governed by the rule of law." Although respect for stare decisis cannot be challenged, "this Court's considered practice [is] not to apply stare decisis as rigidly in constitutional as in nonconstitutional cases." . . . In constitutional questions, where correction depends upon amendment and not upon legislative action this Court throughout its history has freely exercised its power to reexamine the basis of its constitutional decisions."

Even assuming that there is a fundamental right to terminate pregnancy in some situations, there is no justification in law or logic for the trimester framework adopted in *Roe* and employed by the Court today on the basis of stare decisis. For the reasons stated above, that framework is clearly an unworkable means of balancing the fundamental right and the compelling state interests that are indisputably implicated.

The Court in *Roe* correctly realized that the State has important interests "in the areas of health and medical standards" and that "[t]he State has a legitimate interest in seeing to it that abortion, like any other medical procedure, it performed under circumstances that insure maximum safety for the patient." The Court also recognized that the State has "*another* important and legitimate interest in protecting the potentiality of human life." I agree completely that the State has these interests, but in my view, the point at which these interests become compelling does not depend on the trimester of pregnancy. Rather, these interests are present *throughout* pregnancy.

 . . . . It cannot be doubted that as long as a state statute is within "the bounds of reason and [does not] assum[e] the character of a merely arbitrary fiat . . . [then t]he State . . . must decide upon measures that are needful for the protection of its people. . . ." Under the *Roe* framework, however, the state interest in maternal health cannot become compelling until the onset of the second trimester of pregnancy because "until the end of the first trimester mortality in abortion may be less than mortality in normal childbirth." Before the second trimester, the decision to perform an abortion "must be left to the medical judgment of the pregnant woman's attending physician."

The fallacy inherent in the *Roe* framework is apparent: just because the State has a compelling interest in ensuring maternal safety once an abortion may be more dangerous than childbirth, it simply does not follow that the State has no interest before that point that justifies state regulation to ensure that first-trimester abortions are performed as safely as possible.

The state interest in potential human life is likewise extant throughout pregnancy. In *Roe*, the Court held that although the State had an important and legitimate interest in protecting potential life, that interest could not become compelling until the point at which the fetus was viable. The difficulty with this analysis is clear: *potential* life is no less potential in the first weeks of pregnancy than it is at viability or afterward. At any stage in pregnancy, there is the *potential* for human life. Although the Court refused to "resolve the difficult question of when life begins," the Court chose the point of viability - when the fetus is *capable* of life independent of its mother - to permit the complete proscription of abortion. The choice of viability as the point at which the state interest in *potential* life becomes compelling is no less arbitrary than choosing any point before viability or any point afterward. Accordingly, I believe that the State's interest in protecting potential human life exists throughout the pregnancy.

. . . . *"Roe* did not declare an unqualified 'constitutional right to an abortion.' . . . Rather, the right protects the woman from unduly burdensome interference with her

freedom to decide whether to terminate her pregnancy."
The Court and its individual Justices have repeatedly uti-
lized the "unduly burdensome" standard in abortion cases.

. . . . Although the Court does not use the expression
"undue burden," the Court recognizes that even a
"significant obstacle" can be justified by a "reasonable"
regulation.

The "undue burden" required in the abortion cases represents the required threshold inquiry that must be conducted before this Court can require a State to justify its legislative actions under the exacting "compelling state interest" standard. . . .

The "unduly burdensome" standard is particularly appropriate in the abortion context because of the *nature* and
scope of the right that is involved. The privacy right involved in the abortion context "cannot be said to be absolute." "*Roe* did not declare an unqualified 'constitutional
right to an abortion.'" Rather, the *Roe* right is intended to
protect against state action "drastically limiting the availability and safety of the desired service" against the imposition of an "absolute obstacle" on the abortion decision,
or against "official interference" and "coercive restraint"
imposed on the abortion decision. That a state regulation
may "inhibit" abortions to some degree does not require
that we find that the regulation is invalid.

The abortion cases demonstrate that an "undue burden"
has been found for the most part in situations involving
absolute obstacles or severe limitations on the abortion decision. In *Roe*, the Court invalidated a Texas statute that
criminalized *all* abortions except those necessary to save
the life of the mother. In *Danforth*, the Court invalidated

a state prohibition of abortion by saline amniocentesis because the ban had "the effect of inhibiting . . . the vast majority of abortions after the first 12 weeks." The Court today acknowledges that the regulation in *Danforth* effectively represented "a *complete* prohibition on abortions in certain circumstances." In *Danforth*, the Court also invalidated state regulations requiring parental or spousal consent as a prerequisite to a first-trimester abortion because the consent requirements effectively and impermissibly delegated a "veto power" to parents and spouses during the first trimester of pregnancy. In both *Belotti I* and *Belotti v. Baird (Belotti II)*, the Court was concerned with effective parental veto over the abortion decision.

In determining whether the State imposes an "undue burden," we must keep in mind that when we are concerned with extremely sensitive issues, such as the one involved here, "the appropriate forum for their resolution in a democracy is the legislature. We should not forget that 'legislatures are ultimate guardians of the liberties and welfare of the people in quite as great a degree as the courts.' . . .

We must always be mindful that "[t]he Constitution does not compel a state to fine-tune its statutes so as to encourage or facilitate abortions. To the contrary, state action 'encouraging childbirth except in the most urgent circumstances' is 'rationally related to the legitimate governmental objective of protecting potential life.'

Section 1870.03 of the Akron ordinance requires that second-trimester abortions be performed in hospitals. The Court holds that this requirement imposes a "significant obstacle" in the form of increased costs and decreased availability of abortions, and the Court rejects the argument offered by the State that the requirement is a reasonable health regulation under *Roe*.

. . . . I find no justification for the trimester approach
used by the Court to analyze this restriction. I would apply the "unduly burdensome" test and find that the hospitalization requirement does not impose an undue burden
on that decision.

. . . . Health-related factors that may legitimately be considered by the State go well beyond what various medical
organizations have to say about the *physical* safety of a
particular procedure. Indeed, "all factors - physical, emotional, psychological, familial, and the woman's age - [are]
relevant to the well-being of the patient." The ACOG
Standards, upon which the Court relies, state that
"[r]egardless of advances in abortion technology, midtrimester terminations will likely remain more hazardous,
expensive, and emotionally disturbing for a woman than
early abortions."

The hospitalization requirement does not impose an undue
burden, and it is not necessary to apply an exacting standard of review. Further, the regulation has a "rational relation" to a valid state objective of ensuring the health and
welfare of its citizens.

Section 1870.05(B)(2) of the Akron ordinance provides
that no physician shall perform an abortion on a minor
under 15 years of age unless the minor gives written consent, and the physician first obtains the informed written
consent of a parent or guardian, or unless the minor first
obtains "an order from a court having jurisdiction over
her that the abortion be performed or induced." Despite

the fact that this regulation has yet to be [interpreted] in the state courts, the Court holds that the regulation is unconstitutional because it is not "reasonably susceptible of being [interpreted] to create an 'opportunity for case-by-case evaluations of the maturity of pregnant minors.'" I believe that that Court should have abstained from declaring the ordinance unconstitutional.

. . . . Assuming . . . that the Court is correct in holding that a parental notification requirement would be unconstitutional as applied to mature minors, I see no reason to assume that the Akron ordinance and the State Juvenile Court statute compel state judges to notify the parents of a mature minor if such notification was contrary to the minor's best interests. Further, there is no reason to believe that the state courts would construe the consent requirement to impose any type of parental or judicial veto on the abortion decisions of mature minors. In light of the Court's complete lack of knowledge about how the Akron ordinance will operate, and how the Akron ordinance and the State Juvenile Court statute interact, our "'scrupulous regard for the rightful independence of state governments'" counsels against "unnecessary interference by the federal courts with proper and validly administered state concerns, a course so essential to the balanced working of our federal system."

. . . . Despite the fact that the Court finds that Section 1870.06(C) "properly leaves the precise nature and amount of . . . disclosure to the physician's discretion and 'medical judgment,'" the Court also finds Section 1870.06(C) unconstitutional because it requires that the disclosure be made by the attending physician, rather than by other "qualified persons" who work at abortion clinics.

We have approved informed-consent provisions in the past even though the physician was required to deliver certain information to the patient. . . . Indeed, we have held [in earlier cases] that an informed-consent provision does not "unduly burde[n] the right to seek an abortion."

. . . . The remainder of Section 1870.06(B), and Section 1870.06(C), impose no undue burden or drastic limitation on the abortion decision. The city of Akron is merely attempting to ensure that the decision to abort is made in light of that knowledge that the city deems relevant to informed choice. As such, these regulations do not impermissibly affect any privacy right under the Fourteenth Amendment.

Section 1870.07 of the Akron ordinance requires a 24-hour waiting period between the signing of a consent form and the actual performance of the abortion, except in cases of emergency. The court below invalidated this requirement because it affected abortion decisions during the first trimester of pregnancy. The Court affirms [confirms] the decision [of the court] below, not on the ground that it affects early abortions, but because "Akron has failed to demonstrate that any legitimate state interest is furthered by an arbitrary and inflexible waiting period." . . .

It is certainly difficult to understand how the Court believes that the physician-patient relationship is able to accommodate any interest that the State has in maternal physical and mental well-being in light of the fact that the record in this case shows that the relationship is nonexistent. It is also interesting to note that the American College of Obstetricians and Gynecologists recommends that "[p]rior to abortion, the woman should have access to special counseling that explores options for the management of an unwanted pregnancy, examines the risks, and allows sufficient time for reflection prior to making an informed decision."

The waiting period does not apply in cases of medical emergency. Therefore, should the physician determine that the waiting period would increase risks significantly, he or she need not require the woman to wait. The Court's concern in this respect is simply misplaced. Although the waiting period may impose an additional cost on the abortion decision, this increased cost does not unduly burden the availability of abortions or impose an absolute obstacle to access to abortions. Further, the State is not required to "fine-tune" its abortion statutes so as to minimize the costs of abortions.

Assuming . . . that any additional costs are such as to impose an undue burden on the abortion decision, the State's compelling interests in maternal physical and mental health and protection of fetal life clearly justify the waiting period. . . . The waiting period is surely a small cost to impose to ensure that the woman's decision is well considered in light of its certain and irreparable consequences on fetal life, and the possible effects on her own.

Finally, Section 1870.16 of the Akron ordinance requires that "[a]ny physician who shall perform or induce an abortion upon a pregnant woman shall insure that the remains of the unborn child are disposed of in a humane and sanitary manner." The Court finds this provision void for vagueness. I disagree.

. . . . In the present cases, the city of Akron has informed this Court that the intent of the "humane" portion of its statute, as distinguished from the "sanitary" portion, is merely to ensure that fetuses will not be "'dump[ed] . . . on garbage piles.'" In light of the fact that the city of Akron indicates no intent to require that physicians provide "decent burials" for fetuses, and that "humane" is no more vague than the term "sanitary," . . . I cannot conclude that the statute is void for vagueness.

For the reasons set forth above, I dissent from the judgment of the Court in these cases.

PLANNED PARENTHOOD v. ASHCROFT

EXCERPTS

"In weighing the balance between protection of a woman's health and the comparatively small additional cost of a pathologist's examination, we cannot say that the Constitution requires that a State subordinate its interest in health to minimize to this extent the cost of abortions. . . ."

Justice Lewis Powell

"The statute . . . remains impermissibly vague, it fails to inform the physicians whether he may proceed with a postviability abortion in an emergency, or whether he must wait for a second physician even if the woman's life or health will be further imperiled by the delay. This vagueness may well have a severe chilling effect on the physician who perceives the patient's need for a postviability abortion."

Justice Harry Blackmun

In Brief

Question: Are the Missouri abortion statutes unconstitutional?

Lower Court: U.S. District Court, Western Missouri
U.S. Court of Appeals, Eighth Circuit

Law: Missouri Revised Statutes, Section 188.025, etc.

Parties: Planned Parenthood of Kansas City, Missouri
John Ashcroft, Missouri Attorney General

Counsel: For Planned Parenthood: Frank Susman
For Ashcroft: John Ashcroft

Arguments: November 30, 1982

Decision: June 15, 1983

Majority: Chief Justice Burger, Justices Brennan,
Marshall, Blackmun, Powell, Stevens

Minority: Justices White, Rehnquist, O'Connor

Decision by: Justice Powell (p. 109)

Concurrences in part/Dissents in part:

Justice Blackmun (p. 115)
Justice O'Connor (p. 120)

Offical Text: U.S. Reports, Vol. 462, p. 476
Lower Court: Federal Supplement, Vol. 483, p. 679
Federal Reporter 2d, Vol. 655, p. 848

THE ASHCROFT COURT

Chief Justice Warren Burger
Appointed 1969 by Richard M. Nixon

Associate Justice William Brennan
Appointed 1956 by Dwight D. Eisenhower

Associate Justice Byron White
Appointed 1962 by John F. Kennedy

Associate Justice Thurgood Marshall
Appointed 1967 by Lyndon B. Johnson

Associate Justice Harry Blackmun
Appointed 1970 by Richard M. Nixon

Associate Justice Lewis Powell
Appointed 1972 by Richard M. Nixon

Associate Justice William Rehnquist
Appointed 1971 by Richard M. Nixon

Associate Justice John Paul Stevens
Appointed 1975 by Gerald R. Ford

Associate Justice Sandra Day O'Connor
Appointed 1981 by Ronald W. Reagan

PLANNED PARENTHOOD v. ASHCROFT

June 15, 1983

JUSTICE POWELL (joined in part by Chief Justice Burger): [This case], like *City of Akron v. Akron Center for Reproductive Health, Inc.,* and *Simopoulos v. Virginia,* present questions as to the validity of state statutes or local ordinances regulating the performance of abortions.

Planned Parenthood of Kansas City, Missouri, Inc., two physicians who perform abortions, and an abortion clinic (plaintiffs) filed a complaint in the District Court for the Western District of Missouri challenging, as unconstitutional, several sections of the Missouri statutes regulating the performance of abortions. The sections relevant here include Mo Rev Stat Section 188.025, requiring that abortions after 12 weeks of pregnancy be performed in a hospital; Section 188.047, requiring a pathology report for each abortion performed; Section 188.030.3, requiring the presence of a second physician during abortions performed after viability; and Section 188.028, requiring minors to secure parental or judicial consent.

After hearing testimony from a number of expert witnesses, the District Court invalidated all of these sections except the pathology requirement. The Court of Appeals for the Eighth Circuit reversed the District Court's judgment with respect to Section 188.028, thereby upholding the requirement that a minor secure parental or judicial consent to an abortion. It also held that the District Court erred in sustaining [granting] Section 188.047, the pathol-

ogy requirement. The District Court's judgment with respect to the second-physician requirement was affirmed
[confirmed], and the case was remanded [returned to the
lower court] for further proceedings and findings relating
to the second-trimester hospitalization requirement. On
[return], the District Court [confirmed] its holding that
the second-trimester hospitalization requirement was unconstitutional. The Court of Appeals affirmed this judgment. We granted certiorari [agreed to hear the case].

.... In *City of Akron*, we invalidated a city ordinance requiring physicians to perform all second-trimester abortions at general or special hospitals accredited by the Joint
Commission on Accreditation of Hospitals (JCAH) or by
the American Osteopathic Association. Missouri's hospitalization requirements are similar to those enacted by
Akron, as all second-trimester abortions must be performed in general, acute-care facilities. For the reasons
stated in *City of Akron*, we held that such a requirement
"unreasonably infringes upon a woman's constitutional
right to obtain an abortion." For the same reasons, we affirm the Court of Appeals' judgment that Section
188.025 is unconstitutional.

We turn now to the State's second-physician requirement.

In *Roe v. Wade*, the Court recognized that the State has a
compelling interest in the life of a viable fetus. ... Several of the Missouri statutes undertake such regulation.
Postviability abortions are proscribed except when necessary to preserve the life or the health of the woman. The
State also forbids the use of abortion procedures fatal to
the viable fetus unless alternative procedures pose a greater risk to the health of the woman.

The statutory provision at issue in this case requires the attendance of a second physician at the abortion of a viable fetus. This section requires that the second physician "take all reasonable steps in keeping with good medical practice . . . to preserve the life and health of the viable unborn child; provided that it does not pose an increased risk to the life or health of the woman." It also provides that the second physician "shall take control of and provide immediate medical care for a child born as a result of the abortion."

The lower courts invalidated Section 188.030.3. . . .

The first physician's primary concern will be the life and health of the woman. Many third-trimester abortions in Missouri will be emergency operations, as the State permits these late abortions only when they are necessary to preserve the life or the health of the woman. It is not unreasonable for the State to assume that during the operation the first physician's attention and skills will be directed to preserving the woman's health, and not to protecting the actual life of those fetuses who survive the abortion procedure. Viable fetuses will be in immediate and grave danger because of their premature birth. A second physician, in situations where Missouri permits third-trimester abortions, may be of assistance to the woman's physician in preserving the health and life of the child.

By giving immediate medical attention to a fetus that is delivered alive, the second physician will assure that the State's interests are protected more fully than the first physician alone would be able to do. And given the compelling interest that the State has in preserving life, we cannot say that the Missouri requirement of a second physician in those unusual circumstances where Missouri

permits a third-trimester abortion is unconstitutional.
Preserving the life of a viable fetus that is aborted may
not often be possible, but the State legitimately may
choose to provide safeguards for the comparatively few
instances of live birth that occur. We believe the second-
physician requirement reasonably furthers the State's
compelling interest in protecting the lives of viable fetuses, and we reverse the judgment of the Court of Appeals holding that Section 188.030.3 is unconstitutional.

In regulating hospital services within the State, Missouri
requires that "[a]ll tissue surgically removed with the exception of such tissue as tonsils, adenoids, hernial sacs and
prepuces, shall be examined by a pathologist, either on the
premises or by arrangement outside of the hospital."
With respect to abortions, whether performed in hospitals
or in some other facility, Section 188.047 requires the pathologist to "file a copy of the tissue report with the state
division of health. . . ." The pathologist also is required to
"provide a copy of the report to the abortion facility or
hospital in which the abortion was performed or induced."
. . . The narrow question before us is whether the State
lawfully also may require the tissue removed following
abortions performed in clinics as well as in hospitals to be
submitted to a pathologist.

On its face and in effect, Section 188.047 is reasonably
related to generally accepted medical standards and
"further[s] important health-related state concerns." . . .
As a rule, it is accepted medical practice to submit *all* tissue to the examination of a pathologist. This is particularly important following abortion, because questions remain
as to the long-range complications and their effect on subsequent pregnancies. Recorded pathology reports, in con-

cert with abortion complication reports, provide a statistical basis for studying those complications.

. . . . No reason has been suggested why the prudence required in a hospital should not be equally appropriate in such a clinic. Indeed, there may be good reason to impose stricter standards in this respect on clinics performing abortions than on hospitals. . . . There is substantial support for Missouri's requirement. . . .

In weighing the balance between protection of a woman's health and the comparatively small additional cost of a pathologist's examination, we cannot say that the Constitution requires that a State subordinate its interest in health to minimize to this extent the cost of abortions. . . . We think the cost of a tissue examination does not significantly burden a pregnant woman's abortion decision. . . . In *Danforth*, this Court unanimously upheld Missouri's recordkeeping requirement as "useful to the State's interest in protecting the health of its female citizens, and [as] a resource that is relevant to decisions involving medical experience and judgment." We view the requirement for a pathology report as comparable and as a relatively insignificant burden. Accordingly, we reverse the judgment of the Court of Appeals on this issue.

As we noted in *City of Akron*, the relevant legal standards with respect to parental-consent requirements are not in dispute. A State's interest in protecting immature minors will sustain a requirement of a consent substitute, either parental or judicial. It is clear, however, that "the State must provide an alternative procedure whereby a pregnant minor may demonstrate that she is sufficiently mature to make the abortion decision herself or that, despite her immaturity, an abortion would be in her best interests." The issue here is one purely of statutory construction: whether Missouri provides a judicial alternative that is consistent with these established legal standards.

The Missouri statute, Section 188.028.2, in relevant part, provides:

"(4) In the decree, the court shall for good cause:

"(a) Grant the petition for majority rights for the purpose of consenting to the abortion; or

"(b) Find the abortion to be in the best interests of the minor and give judicial consent to the abortion, setting forth the grounds for so finding; or

"(c) Deny the petition, setting forth the grounds on which the petition is denied."

On its face, Section 188.028.2(4) authorizes Juvenile Courts to choose among any of the alternatives outlined in the section. The Court of Appeals concluded that a denial of the petition permitted in subsection (c) "would initially require the court to find that the minor was not emancipated and was not mature enough to make her own decision and that an abortion was not in her best interests." [Planned Parenthood] contend[s] that this interpretation is unreasonable. We do not agree.

Where fairly possible, courts should construe a statute to avoid a danger of unconstitutionality. The Court of Appeals was aware, if the Statute provides discretion to deny permission to a minor for *any* "good cause," that arguably it would violate the principles that this Court has set forth. It recognized, however, that before exercising any option, the Juvenile Court must receive evidence on "the emotional development, maturity, intellect and understanding of the minor." The court then reached the logical conclusion that "findings and the ultimate denial of the petition must be supported by a showing of 'good cause.'" The Court of Appeals reasonably found that a court could not deny a petition "for good cause" unless it first found - after having received the required evidence - that the minor was not mature enough to make her own decision. We conclude that the Court of Appeals correctly interpreted the statute and that Section 188.028, as interpreted, avoids any constitutional infirmities.

The judgment of the Court of Appeals, insofar as it invalidated Missouri's second-trimester hospitalization requirement and upheld the State's parental- and judicial-consent provision, is affirmed. The judgment invalidating the requirement of a pathology report for all abortions and the requirement that a second physician attend the abortion of any viable fetus is reversed. . . .

It is so ordered.

JUSTICE BLACKMUN (joined by Justices Brennan, Marshall, and Stevens), concurring in part and dissenting in part: The Court's decision today in *Akron v. Akron Center for Reproductive Health, Inc.*, invalidates the city of Akron's hospitalization requirement and a host of other provisions that infringe on a woman's decision to terminate her pregnancy through abortion. I agree that Missouri's hospitalization requirement is invalid under the *Akron* analysis. . . . I do not agree, however, that the remaining Missouri statutes challenged . . . satisfy the constitutional standards set forth in *Akron* and the Court's prior decisions.

Missouri law provides that whenever an abortion is performed, a tissue sample must be submitted to a "board eligible or certified pathologist" for a report. This requirement applies to first-trimester abortions as well as to
those performed later in pregnancy. Our past decisions
establish that the performance of abortions during the
first trimester must be left "'free of interference by the
State.'" As we have noted in *Akron*, this does not mean
that every regulation touching upon first-trimester abortions is constitutionally impermissible. But to pass constitutional muster, regulations affecting first-trimester abortions must "have no significant impact on the woman's exercise of her right" and must be "justified by important
state health objectives."

Missouri's requirement of a pathologist's report is not justified by important health objectives. Although pathology
examinations may be "useful and even necessary in some
cases," Missouri requires more than a pathology examination and a pathology report; it demands that the examination be performed and the report prepared by a "board eligible or certified pathologist" rather than by the attending physician. Contrary to Justice Powell's assertion, this
requirement of a report by a pathologist is not in accord
with "generally accepted medical standards." The routine
and accepted medical practice is for the attending physician to perform a gross (visual) examination of any tissue
removed during an abortion. Only if the physician detects
abnormalities is there a need to send a tissue sample to a
pathologist. The American College of Obstetricians and
Gynecologists (ACOG) does not recommend an examination by a pathologist in every case. . . .

Nor does the National Abortion Federation believe that
such an examination is necessary. . . .

While a pathologist may be better able to perform a microscopic examination, Missouri law does not require a microscopic examination unless "fetal parts or placenta are not identified." Thus, the effect of the Missouri statute is to require a pathologist to perform the initial gross examination, which is normally the responsibility of the attending physician and which will often make the pathologist's services unnecessary.

. . . . I must conclude that the State has not "met its burden of demonstrating that [the pathologist requirement] further[s] important health-related State concerns." There has been no showing that tissue examinations by a pathologist do more to protect health than examinations by a nonpathologist physician. Missouri does not require pathologists' reports for any other surgical procedures performed in clinics, or for minor surgery performed in hospitals. Moreover, I cannot agree with Justice Powell that Missouri's pathologist requirement has "no significant impact" on a woman's exercise of her right to an abortion. It is undisputed that this requirement may increase the cost of a first-trimester abortion by as much as $40. Although this increase may seem insignificant from the Court's comfortable perspective, I cannot say that it is equally insignificant to every woman seeking an abortion. For the woman on welfare or the unemployed teenager, this additional cost may well put the price of an abortion beyond reach.

. . . . Missouri's requirement of a pathologist's report unquestionably adds significantly to the cost of providing abortions, and Missouri has not shown that it serves any substantial health-related purpose. Under these circumstances, I would hold that constitutional limits have been exceeded.

In Missouri, an abortion may be performed after viability only if necessary to preserve the life or health of the woman. When a postviability abortion is performed, Missouri law provides that "there [must be] in attendance a [second] physician . . . who shall take control of and provide immediate medical care for a child born as a result of the abortion." . . .

While I agree that a second physician indeed may aid in preserving the life of a fetus born alive, this type of aid is possible only when the abortion method used is one that may result in a live birth. Although Missouri ordinarily requires a physician performing a postviability abortion to use the abortion method most likely to preserve fetal life, this restriction does not apply when this method "would present a greater risk to the life and health of the woman."

. . . . When a D&E [dilation and evacuation] abortion is performed, the second physician can do nothing to further the State's compelling interest in protecting potential life. His presence is superfluous. The second-physician requirement thus is overbroad and "imposes a burden on women in cases where the burden is not justified by any possibility of survival of the fetus."

. . . . The choice of method presumably will be made in advance, and any need for a second physician disappears when the woman's health requires that the choice be D&E. Because the statute is not tailored to protect the State's legitimate interests, I would hold it invalid.

In addition, I would hold that the statute's failure to provide a clear exception for emergency situations renders it unconstitutional. . . . By requiring the attendance of a second physician even when the resulting delay may be harmful to the health of the pregnant woman, the statute impermissibly fails to make clear "that the woman's life and health must always prevail over the fetus' life and health when they conflict."

. . . . The statute . . . remains impermissibly vague; it fails to inform the physician whether he may proceed with a postviability abortion in an emergency, or whether he must wait for a second physician even if the woman's life or health will be further imperiled by the delay. This vagueness may well have a severe chilling effect on the physician who perceives the patient's need for a postviability abortion. In *Colautti v. Franklin*, we considered a statute that failed to specify whether it "require[d] the physician to make a 'trade-off' between the woman's health and additional percentage points of fetal survival." The Court held there that "where conflicting duties of this magnitude are involved, the State, at the least, must proceed with greater precision before it may subject a physician to possible criminal sanctions." I would apply that reasoning here, and hold Missouri's second-physician requirement invalid on this ground as well.

Missouri law prohibits the performance of an abortion on an unemancipated minor absent parental consent or a court order.

Until today, the Court has never upheld "a requirement of a consent substitute, either parental or judicial." . . .

I continue to adhere to the views expressed by Justice Stevens in *Belotti II.*

"It is inherent in the right to make the abortion decision that the right may be exercised without public
scrutiny and in defiance of the contrary opinion of the
sovereign or other third parties. . . . [T]he only standard provided for the judge's decision is the best interest of the minor. That standard provides little real
guidance to the judge, and his decision must necessarily
reflect personal and societal values and mores whose
enforcement upon the minor - particularly when contrary to her own informed and reasonable decision - is
fundamentally at odds with privacy interests underlying the constitutional protection afforded to her decision."

Because Mo Rev State Section 188.028 permits a parental or judicial veto of a minor's decision to obtain
an abortion, I would hold it unconstitutional.

JUSTICE O'CONNOR (joined by Justices White and
Rehnquist), concurring in part in the judgment and dissenting in part: . . . I believe that the second-trimester
hospitalization requirement imposed by Section
188.025 does not impose an undue burden on the limited right to undergo an abortion. Assuming [for the
sake of argument] that the requirement was an undue
burden, it would nevertheless "reasonably relat[e] to
the preservation and protection of maternal health." I
therefore dissent from the Court's judgment that the
requirement is unconstitutional.

I agree that the second-physician requirement contained in Section 188.030.3 is constitutional because
the State possesses a compelling interest in protecting
and preserving fetal life, but I believe that this state in-

terest is extant throughout pregnancy. I therefore concur in the judgment of the Court.

I agree that the pathology-report requirement imposed by Section 188.047 is constitutional because it imposes no undue burden on the limited right to undergo an abortion. Because I do not believe that the validity of this requirement is contingent in any way on the trimester of pregnancy in which it is imposed, I concur in the judgment of the Court.

Assuming [for the sake of argument] that the State cannot impose a parental veto on the decision of a minor to undergo an abortion, I agree that the parental-consent provision contained in Section 188.028 is constitutional. However, I believe that the provision is valid because it imposes no undue burden on any right that a minor may have to undergo an abortion. I concur in the judgment of the Court on this issue. . . .

SIMOPOULOS v. VIRGINIA

EXCERPTS

"We consistently have recognized and reaffirm today that a State has an 'important and legitimate interest in the health of the mother' that becomes '"compelling"' . . . at approximately the end of the first trimester.'"

"P.M. went to a motel. Alone, she aborted her fetus in the motel bathroom 48 hours after the saline injection. She left the fetus, follow-up instructions, and pain medication in the wastebasket at the motel. Her boy friend took her home. Police found the fetus later that day and began an investigation."

Justice Lewis Powell

In Brief

Question:	Is Virginia's mandatory hospitalization requirement for second trimester abortions constitutional?
Lower Court:	Virginia Supreme Court
Law:	Virginia Code, Section 18.2-71 et seq. (1982)
Parties:	Chris Simopoulos, a physician The State of Virginia
Counsel:	For Simopoulos: Roy Lucas For Virginia: William Broaddus
Arguments:	November 30, 1982
Decision:	June 15, 1983
Majority:	Chief Justice Burger, Justices Brennan, Marshall, Blackmun, Powell
Minority:	Justices White, Rehnquist, Stevens, O'Connor
Decision by:	Justice Powell (p. 127)
Concurrences:	Justice O'Connor (p. 131)
Dissents:	Justice Stevens (p. 132)
Offical Text:	U.S. Reports, Vol. 462, p. 506
Lower Court:	Virginia Reports, Vol. 221, p. 1059

THE SIMOPOULOS COURT

Chief Justice Warren Burger
Appointed 1969 by Richard M. Nixon

Associate Justice William Brennan
Appointed 1956 by Dwight D. Eisenhower

Associate Justice Byron White
Appointed 1962 by John F. Kennedy

Associate Justice Thurgood Marshall
Appointed 1967 by Lyndon B. Johnson

Associate Justice Harry Blackmun
Appointed 1970 by Richard M. Nixon

Associate Justice Lewis Powell
Appointed 1972 by Richard M. Nixon

Associate Justice William Rehnquist
Appointed 1971 by Richard M. Nixon

Associate Justice John Paul Stevens
Appointed 1975 by Gerald R. Ford

Associate Justice Sandra Day O'Connor
Appointed 1981 by Ronald W. Reagan

SIMOPOULOS v. VIRGINIA

June 15, 1983

JUSTICE POWELL: .... The principal issue here is whether Virginia's mandatory hospitalization requirement is constitutional.

Appellant [Simopoulos] is a practicing obstetrician-gynecologist certified by the American Board of Obstetrics and Gynecology. In November 1979, he practiced at his office in Woodbridge, Virginia, at four local hospitals, and at his clinic in Falls Church, Virginia. The Falls Church clinic has an operating room and facilities for resuscitation and emergency treatment of cardiac-respiratory arrest. Replacement and stabilization fluids are on hand. [Simopoulos] customarily performs first-trimester abortions at his clinic. During the time relevant to this case, the clinic was not licensed, nor had [Simopoulos] sought any license for it.

P.M. was a 17-year-old high school student when she went to [Simopoulos'] clinic on November 8, 1979. She was unmarried, and told [Simopoulos] that she was approximately 22 weeks pregnant. She requested an abortion but did not want her parents to know. Examination by [Simopoulos] confirmed that P.M. was five months pregnant, well into the second trimester. [Simopoulos] testified that he encouraged her to confer with her parents and discussed with her the alternative of continuing the pregnancy to term. She did return home, but never advised her parents of her decision.

Two days later, P.M. returned to the clinic with her boy friend. The abortion was performed by an injection of saline solution. P.M. told [Simopoulos] that she planned to deliver the fetus in a motel, and understood him to agree to this course. [Simopoulos] gave P.M. a prescription for an analgesic and a "Post-Injection Information" sheet that stated that she had undergone "a surgical procedure" and warned of a "wide range of normal reactions." The sheet also advised that she call the physician if "heavy" bleeding began. Although P.M. did not recall being advised to go to a hospital when labor began, this was included on the instruction sheet.

P.M. went to a motel. Alone, she aborted her fetus in the motel bathroom 48 hours after the saline injection. She left the fetus, follow-up instructions, and pain medication in the wastebasket at the motel. Her boy friend took her home. Police found the fetus later that day and began an investigation.

[Simopoulos] was indicted for unlawfully performing an abortion during the second trimester of pregnancy outside of a licensed hospital and was convicted by the Circuit Court of Fairfax County sitting without a jury. The Supreme Court of Virginia unanimously affirmed [confirmed] the conviction. This appeal followed....

We consistently have recognized and reaffirm today that a State has an "important and legitimate interest in the health of the mother" that becomes "'compelling' . . . at approximately the end of the first trimester." This interest embraces the facilities and circumstances in which abortions are performed. [Simopoulos] argues, however, that Virginia prohibits all nonhospital second-trimester abortions and that such a requirement imposes an unconstitutional burden on the right of privacy. In *City of Akron* and *Ashcroft*, we upheld such a constitutional challenge to the acute-care hospital requirements at issue there. The State of Virginia argues here that its hospitalization requirements differs significantly from the hospitalization requirements considered in *City of Akron* and *Ashcroft* and that it reasonably promotes the State's interests.

In furtherance of its compelling interest in maternal health, Virginia has enacted a hospitalization requirement for abortions performed during the second trimester. As a general proposition, physicians' offices are not regulated under Virginia law. Virginia law does not, however, permit a physician licensed in the practice of medicine and surgery to perform an abortion during the second trimester of pregnancy unless "such procedure is performed in a hospital licensed by the State Department of Health." The Virginia abortion statute itself does not define the term "hospital." This definition is found in Va Code Section 32.1.123.1 that defines "hospital" to include "outpatient . . . hospitals." Section 20.2.11 of the Department of Health's Rules and Regulations for the Licensure of Outpatient Hospitals in Virginia defines "outpatient hospitals" in pertinent part as "[i]nstitutions . . . which primarily provide facilities for the performance of surgical procedures on outpatients" and provides that second-trimester abortions may be performed in these clinics. Thus, under Virginia law, a second-trimester abortion may be performed in an outpatient surgical hospital provided that facility has been licensed as a "hospital" by the State.

. . . . In contrast [to the *City of Akron* and *Ashcroft*], the Virginia statutes and regulations do not require that second-trimester abortions be performed exclusively in full-service hospitals. Under Virginia's hospitalization requirement,outpatient surgical hospitals may qualify for licensing as "hospitals" in which second-trimester abortions lawfully may be performed. Thus, our decisions in *City of Akron* and *Ashcroft* are not controlling here.

In view of its interest in protecting the health of its citizens, the State necessarily has considerable discretion in determining standards for the licensing of medical facilities. Although its discretion does not permit it to adopt abortion regulations that depart from accepted medical practice, it does have a legitimate interest in regulating second-trimester abortions and setting forth the standards for facilities in which such abortions are performed.

On their face, the Virginia regulations appear to be generally compatible with accepted medical standards governing outpatient second-trimester abortions. . . . The medical profession has not thought that a State's standards need be relaxed merely because the facility performs abortions: "Ambulatory care facilities providing abortion services should meet the same standards of care as those recommended for other surgical procedures performed in the physician's office and outpatient clinic or the freestanding and hospital-based ambulatory setting." . . . Indeed, the medical profession's standards for outpatient surgical facilities are stringent: "Such facilities should maintain the same surgical, anesthetic, and personnel standards as recommended for hospitals."

. . . . [Simopoulos'] challenge throughout this litigation appears to have been limited to an assertion that the State cannot require all second-trimester abortions to be performed in full-service general hospitals. . . . We can only assume that by continuing to challenge the Virginia hospitalization requirement [Simopoulos] either views the Virginia regulations in some unspecified way as unconstitu-

tional or challenges a hospitalization requirement that doe
not exist in Virginia. Yet, not until his reply brief in this
Court did he elect to criticize the regulations apart from
his broadside attack on the entire Virginia hospitalization
requirement.

Given the plain language of the Virginia regulations and
the history of their adoption, we see no reason to doubt
that an adequately equipped clinic could, upon proper application, obtain an outpatient hospital license permitting
the performance of second-trimester abortions. We conclude that Virginia's requirement that second-trimester
abortions be performed in licensed clinics is not an unreasonable means of furthering the State's compelling interest in "protecting the woman's own health and safety." As
we emphasized in *Roe*, "[t]he State has a legitimate interest in seeing to it that abortion, like any other medical
procedure, is performed under circumstances that insure
maximum safety for the patient." Unlike the provisions
at issue in *City of Akron* and *Ashcroft*, Virginia's statute
and regulations do not require that the patient be hospital-
ized as an inpatient or that the abortion be performed in a
full-service, acute-care hospital.   Rather, the State's requirement that second-trimester abortions be performed
in licensed clinics appears to comport with accepted medical practice, and leaves the method and timing of the
abortion precisely where they belong - with the physician
and the patient.

The judgment of the Supreme Court of Virginia is affirmed.

JUSTICE O'CONNOR (joined by Justices White and
Rehnquist), concurring in part and concurring in the judgment: . . . . I concur in the judgment of the Court insofar

as it affirms [confirms] the conviction. . . . I do not agree
that the constitutional validity of the Virginia mandatory
hospitalization requirement is contingent in any way on
the trimester in which it is imposed. Rather, I believe that
the requirement in this case is not an undue burden on the
decision to undergo an abortion.

JUSTICE STEVENS, dissenting: Prior to this Court's decision in *Roe v. Wade*, it was a felony to perform any abortion in Virginia except in a hospital accredited by the
Joint Committee on Accreditation of Hospitals and licensed by the Department of Health, and with the approval of the hospital's Abortion Review Board (a committee
of three physicians). In 1975, the Virginia Code was
amended to authorize additional abortions, including any
second-trimester abortion performed by a physician "in a
hospital licensed by the State Department of Health or under the control of the State Board of Mental Health and
Mental Retardation."

The amended statute might be interpreted in either of two
ways. It might be read to prohibit all second-trimester
abortions except those performed in a full-service, acute-
care hospital facility. Or it might be read to permit any
abortion performed in a facility licensed as a "hospital" in
accord with any regulations subsequently adopted by the
Department of Health. The Court today chooses the latter
interpretation.

There is reason to think the Court may be wrong. At the
time the statute was enacted, there were no regulations
identifying abortion clinics as "hospitals." The structure
of the 1975 amendment suggests that the Virginia General Assembly did not want to make any greater change in
its law than it believed necessary to comply with *Roe v.*

Wade, and it may well have thought a full-service, acute-care hospitalization requirement constitutionally acceptable. . . . The opinion [of the Supreme Court of Virginia] refers to "clinics" only once, as part of a general statement concerning the variety of medical care facilities the State licenses and regulates; even there, the term is included in the list as a category that is distinct from "hospitals."

On the other hand, the Court may well be correct in its interpretation of the Virginia statute. The word "hospital" in Section 18.2-73 could incorporate by reference any institution licensed in accord with Va Code Section 32.1-123.1 and its implementing regulations. It is not this Court's role, however, to interpret state law. We should not rest our decision on an interpretation of state law that was not endorsed by the court whose judgment we are reviewing. The Virginia Supreme Court's opinion was written on the assumption that the Commonwealth could constitutionally require all second-trimester abortions to be performed in a full-service, acute-care hospital. Our decision today in *City of Akron v. Akron Center for Reproductive Health, Inc.*, proves that assumption to have been incorrect. The proper disposition of this appeal is therefore to vacate [annul] the judgment of the Supreme Court of Virginia and to remand [return] the case to that court to reconsider its holding in the light of our opinion in *Akron.*

I respectfully dissent.

THORNBURGH v.
AMERICAN COLLEGE

EXCERPTS

"Few decisions are more personal and intimate, more properly private, or more basic to individual dignity and autonomy, than a woman's decision - with the guidance of her physician and within the limits specified in *Roe* - whether to end her pregnancy. A woman's right to make that choice freely is fundamental. Any other result, in our view, would protect inadequately a central part of the sphere of liberty that our law guarantees equally to all."

"We note, as we reach this conclusion, that the Court consistently has refused to allow government to chill the exercise of constitutional rights by requiring disclosure of protected, but sometimes unpopular, activities. Pennsylvania's reporting requirements raise the specter of public exposure and harassment of women who choose to exercise their personal, intensely private, right, with their physician, to end a pregnancy. Thus, they pose an unacceptable danger of deterring the exercise of that right, and must be invalidated."

Justice Harry Blackmun

In Brief

Question: Is the Pennsylvania Abortion Control Act unconstitutional?

Lower Court: U.S. District Court, Eastern Pennsylvania
U.S. Court of Appeals, Third Circuit

Law: Pennsylvania Abortion Control Act (1982)

Parties: Richard Thornburgh, Governor, Pennsylvania
American College of Obstetricians
& Gynecologists

Counsel: For Thornburgh: Andrew Gordon
For American College: Kathryn Kolbert

Arguments: November 5, 1985

Decision: June 11, 1986

Majority: Justices Brennan, Marshall, Blackmun, Powell, Stevens

Minority: Chief Justice Burger, Justices White, Rehnquist, O'Connor

Decision by: Justice Blackmun (p. 139)

Concurrences: Justice Stevens (p. 148)

Dissents: Chief Justice Burger (p. 151)
Justice White (p. 154)
Justice O'Connor (p. 169)

Offical Text: U.S. Reports, Vol. 476, p. 747
Lower Court: Federal Supplement, Vol. 552, p. 791
Federal Reporter 2d, Vol. 737, P. 283

THE THORNBURGH COURT

Chief Justice Warren Burger
Appointed 1969 by Richard M. Nixon

Associate Justice William Brennan
Appointed 1956 by Dwight D. Eisenhower

Associate Justice Byron White
Appointed 1962 by John F. Kennedy

Associate Justice Thurgood Marshall
Appointed 1967 by Lyndon B. Johnson

Associate Justice Harry Blackmun
Appointed 1970 by Richard M. Nixon

Associate Justice Lewis Powell
Appointed 1972 by Richard M. Nixon

Associate Justice William Rehnquist
Appointed 1971 by Richard M. Nixon

Associate Justice John Paul Stevens
Appointed 1975 by Gerald R. Ford

Associate Justice Sandra Day O'Connor
Appointed 1981 by Ronald W. Reagan

THORNBURGH v.
AMERICAN COLLEGE

June 11, 1986

JUSTICE BLACKMUN: This is an appeal from a judgment of the United States Court of Appeals for the Third Circuit. . . . The Court of Appeals held unconstitutional several provisions of Pennsylvania's current Abortion Control Act. . . .

The Abortion Control Act was approved by the Governor of the Commonwealth on June 11, 1982. By its own terms, however, it was to become effective only 180 days thereafter, that is, on the following December 8. It had been offered as an amendment to a pending bill to regulate paramilitary training.

The 1982 Act was not the Commonwealth's first attempt, after this Court's 1973 decisions in *Roe v. Wade* and *Doe v. Bolton*, to impose abortion restraints. The State's first post-1973 Abortion Control Act was passed in 1974 over the Governor's veto. After extensive litigation, various provisions of the 1974 statute were ruled unconstitutional, including those relating to spousal or parental consent, to the choice of procedure for a postviability abortion, and to the proscription of abortion advertisements.

In 1978, the Pennsylvania Legislature attempted to restrict access to abortion by limiting medical-assistance funding for the procedure. This effort, too, was successfully challenged in federal court, and that judgment was affirmed [confirmed] by the Third Circuit.

In 1981, abortion legislation was proposed in the Pennsylvania House as an amendment to a pending Senate bill to
outlaw "tough-guy competitions." The suggested amendment, aimed at limiting abortions, was patterned after a
model statute developed by a Chicago-based, nonprofit anti-abortion organization. The bill underwent further
change in the legislative process but, when passed, was
vetoed by the Governor. Finally, the 1982 Act was for-
mulated, enacted, and approved.

After the passage of the Act, but before its effective
date, the present litigation was instituted in the United
States District Court for the Eastern District of Pennsylvania. . . .

This case, as it comes to us, concerns the constitutionality
of six provisions of the Pennsylvania Act that the Court
of Appeals struck down as facially invalid: Section 3205
("informed   consent");   Section   3208   ("printed
information"); Sections 3214(a) and (h) (reporting requirements); Section 3211(a) (determination of viability);
Section 3210(b) (degree of care required in postviability
abortions); and Section 3210(c) (second-physician requirement). We have no reason to address the validity of the
other sections of the Act challenged in the District Court.

Less than three years ago, this Court, in *Akron, Ashcroft,*
and *Simopoulos,* reviewed challenges to state and munici-
pal legislation regulating the performance of abortions.
In *Akron,* the Court specifically reaffirmed *Roe v. Wade.*
Again today, we reaffirm the general principles laid down
in *Roe* and in *Akron.*

In the years since this Court's decision in *Roe,* States and
municipalities have adopted a number of measures seem-

ingly designed to prevent a woman, with the advice of her physician, from exercising her freedom of choice. Akron is but one example. But the constitutional principles that led this Court to its decisions in 1973 still provide the compelling reason for recognizing the constitutional dimensions of a woman's right to decide whether to end her pregnancy. "[I]t should go without saying that the vitality of these constitutional principles cannot be allowed to yield simply because of disagreement with them." The States are not free, under the guise of protecting maternal health or potential life, to intimidate women into continuing pregnancies. [Thornburgh] claim[s] that the statutory provisions before us today further legitimate compelling interests of the Commonwealth. Close analysis of those provisions, however, shows that they wholly subordinate constitutional privacy interests and concerns with maternal health in an effort to deter a woman from making a decision that, with her physician, is hers to make.

. . . . Section 3205(a) requires that the woman give her "voluntary and informed consent" to an abortion. Failure to observe the provisions of Section 3205 subjects the physician to suspension or revocation of his license, and subjects any other person obligated to provide information relating to informed consent to criminal penalties. A requirement that the woman give what is truly a voluntary and informed consent, as a general proposition, is, of course, proper and is surely not unconstitutional. But the State may not require the delivery of information designed "to influence the woman's informed choice between abortion or childbirth."

. . . . Sections 3205 and 3208 . . . prescribe in detail the method for securing "informed consent." Seven explicit kinds of information must be delivered to the woman at

least 24 hours before her consent is given, and five of
these must be presented by the woman's physician. The
five are: (a) the name of the physician who will perform
the abortion, (b) the "fact that there may be detrimental
physical and psychological effects which are not accurate-
ly foreseeable," (c) the "particular medical risks associated
with the particular abortion procedure to be employed,"
(d) the probable gestational age, and (e) the "medical risks
associated with carrying her child to term." The remaining two categories are (f) the "fact that medical assistance
benefits may be available for prenatal care, childbirth and
neonatal care," and (g) the "fact that the father is liable to
assist" in the child's support, "even in instances where the
father has offered to pay for the abortion." The woman
also must be informed that materials printed and supplied
by the Commonwealth that describe the fetus and that list
agencies offering alternatives to abortion are available for
her review. If she chooses to review the materials but is
unable to read, the materials "shall be read to her," and
any answer she seeks must be "provided her in her own
language." She must certify in writing, prior to the abortion, that all this has been done. The printed materials
"shall include the following statement":

"'There are many public and private agencies willing
and able to help you to carry your child to term, and to
assist you and your child after your child is born,
whether you choose to keep your child or place her or
him for adoption. The Commonwealth of Pennsylvania
strongly urges you to contact them before making a final decision about abortion. The law requires that your
physician or his agent give you the opportunity to call
agencies like these before you undergo an abortion.'"

The materials must describe the "probable anatomical and physiological characteristics of the unborn child at two-week gestational increments from fertilization to full term, including any relevant information on the possibility of the unborn child's survival."

. . . . The informational requirements in the Akron ordinance were invalid for two "equally decisive" reasons. The first was that "much of the information required is designed not to inform the woman's consent but rather to persuade her to withhold it altogether." The second was that a rigid requirement that a specific body of information be given in all cases, irrespective of the particular needs of the patient, intrudes upon the discretion of the pregnant woman's physician and thereby imposes the "undesired and uncomfortable straitjacket" with which the Court in *Danforth* was concerned.

These two reasons apply with equal and controlling force to the specific and intrusive informational prescriptions of the Pennsylvania statutes. The printed materials required by Sections 3205 and 3208 seem to us to be nothing less than an outright attempt to wedge the Commonwealth's message discouraging abortion into the privacy of the informed-consent dialogue between the woman and her physician. . . .

Under the guise of informed consent, the Act requires the dissemination of information that is not relevant to such consent, and, thus, it advances no legitimate state interest. The requirements of Sections 3205(a)(1)(ii) and (iii) that the woman be informed by the physician of "detrimental physical and psychological effects" and of all "particular medical risks" compound the problem of medical attendance, increase the patient's anxiety, and intrude upon the physician's exercise of proper professional judgment. This type of compelled information is the antithesis of informed consent. . . . Pennsylvania, like Akron, "has gone far beyond merely describing the general subject matter relevant to informed consent." . . . Section 3205's informational requirements therefore are facially unconstitutional.

. . . . *Sections 3214(a) and (h) (reporting) and Section 3211(a) (determination of viability).* Section 3214(a)(8), part of the general reporting section, incorporates Section 3211(a). Section 3211(a) requires the physician to report the basis for his determination "that a child is not viable." It applies only after the first trimester. The report required by Sections 3214(a) and (h) is detailed and must include, among other things, identification of the performing and referring physicians and of the facility or agency; information as to the woman's political subdivision and State of residence, age, race, marital status, and number of prior pregnancies; the date of her last menstrual period and the probable gestational age; the basis for any judgment that a medical emergency existed; the basis for any determination of nonviability; and the method of payment for the abortion. The report is to be signed by the attending physician.

Despite the fact that Section 3214(e)(2) provides that such reports "shall not be deemed public records," within the meaning of the Commonwealth's "Right to Know Law," each report "shall be made available for public inspection and copying within 15 days of receipt in a form which will not lead to the disclosure of the identity of any person filing a report." Similarly, the report of complications, required by Section 3214(h), "shall be open to public inspection and copying." A willful failure to file a re-

port required under Section 3214 is "unprofessional conduct" and the noncomplying physician's license "shall be
subject to suspension or revocation."

The scope of the information required and its availability
to the public belie any assertions by the Commonwealth
that it is advancing any legitimate interest. In *Planned
Parenthood of Central Missouri v. Danforth*, we recognized that recordkeeping and reporting provisions "that
are reasonably directed to the preservation of maternal
health and that properly respect a patient's confidentiality
and privacy are permissible." But the reports required under the Act before us today go well beyond the health-
related interests that served to justify the Missouri reports
under consideration in *Danforth*. . . .

The elements that proved persuasive for the ruling in
Danforth are absent here. The decision to terminate a
pregnancy is an intensely private one that must be protected in a way that assures anonymity. . . .

A woman and her physician will necessarily be more re-
luctant to choose an abortion if there exists a possibility
that her decision and her identity will become known
publicly. Although the statute does not specifically require the reporting of the woman's name, the amount of
information about her and the circumstances under which
she had an abortion are so detailed that identification is
likely. Identification is the obvious purpose of these extreme reporting requirements. The "impermissible limits"
that *Danforth* mentioned and that Missouri approached
have been exceeded here.

We note, as we reach this conclusion, that the Court consistently has refused to allow government to chill the ex-

ercise of constitutional rights by requiring disclosure of
protected, but sometimes unpopular, activities. Pennsylvania's reporting requirements raise the specter of public
exposure and harassment of women who choose to exercise their personal, intensely private, right, with their
physician, to end a pregnancy. Thus, they pose an unacceptable danger of deterring the exercise of that right,
and must be invalidated.

*Section 3210(b) (degree of care for postviability abor-
tions) and Section 3210(c) (second-physician requirement
when the fetus is possibly viable).* Section 3210(b) sets
forth two independent requirements for a post-viability
abortion. First, it demands the exercise of that degree of
care "which such person would be required to exercise in
order to preserve the life and health of any unborn child
intended to be born and not aborted." Second, "the abortion technique employed shall be that which would provide the best opportunity for the unborn child to be
aborted alive unless," in the physician's good-faith judgment, that technique "would present a significantly greater medical risk to the life or health of the pregnant woman." An intentional, knowing, or reckless violation of this
standard is a felony of the third degree, and subjects the
violator to the possibility of imprisonment for not more
than seven years and to a fine of not more than $15,000.

The Court of Appeals ruled that Section 3210(b) was unconstitutional because it required a "trade-off" between
the woman's health and fetal survival, and failed to require that maternal health be the physician's paramount
consideration. . . .

We agree with the Court of Appeals and therefore find
the statute to be facially invalid.

Section 3210(c) requires that a second physician be present during an abortion performed when viability is possible. The second physician is to "take control of the child and . . . provide immediate medical care for the child, taking all reasonable steps necessary, in his judgment, to preserve the child's life and health." Violation of this requirement is a felony of the third degree.

. . . . Section 3210(c) of the Pennsylvania statute contains no express exception for an emergency situation. . . . Pennsylvania's statute contains no such comforting or helpful language and evinces no intent to protect a woman whose life may be at risk. Section 3210(a) provides only a defense to criminal liability for a physician who concluded, in good faith, that a fetus was nonviable "or that the abortion was necessary to preserve maternal life or health." It does not relate to the second-physician requirement and its words are not words of emergency.

It is clear that the Pennsylvania Legislature knows how to provide a medical-emergency exception when it chooses to do so. It defined "[m]edical emergency" in general terms in Section 3203, and it specifically provided a medical-emergency exception with respect to informational requirements, Section 3205(b); for parental consent, Section 3206; for post-first-trimester hospitalization, Section 3209; and for a public official's issuance of an order for an abortion without the express voluntary consent of the woman, Section 3215(f). We necessarily conclude that the legislature's failure to provide a medical-emergency exception in Section 3210(c) was intentional. All the factors are here for chilling the performance of a late abortion, which, more than one performed at an earlier date, perhaps tends to be under emergency conditions.

Constitutional rights do not always have easily ascertainable boundaries, and controversy over the meaning of our Nation's most majestic guarantees frequently has been turbulent. As judges, however, we are sworn to uphold the law even when its content gives rise to bitter dispute. We recognized at the very beginning of our opinion in *Roe* that abortion raises moral and spiritual questions over which honorable persons can disagree sincerely and profoundly. But those disagreements did not then and do not now relieve us of our duty to apply the Constitution faithfully.

Our cases long have recognized that the Constitution embodies a promise that a certain private sphere of individual liberty will be kept largely beyond the reach of government. That promise extends to women as well as to men. Few decisions are more personal and intimate, more properly private, or more basic to individual dignity and autonomy, than a woman's decision - with the guidance of her physician and within the limits specified in *Roe* - whether to end her pregnancy. A woman's right to make that choice freely is fundamental. Any other result, in our view, would protect inadequately a central part of the sphere of liberty that our law guarantees equally to all.

The Court of Appeals correctly invalidated the specified provisions of Pennsylvania's 1982 Abortion Control Act. Its judgment is affirmed [confirmed].

It is so ordered.

JUSTICE STEVENS, concurring: The scope of the individual interest in liberty that is given protection by the Due Process Clause of the Fourteenth Amendment is a

matter about which conscientious judges have long disa-
greed. . . .

[T]he aspect of liberty at stake in this case is the freedom
from unwarranted governmental intrusion into individual
decisions in matters of childbearing. As Justice White explained in *Griswold,* that aspect of liberty comes to this
Court with a momentum for respect that is lacking when
appeal is made to liberties which derive merely from
shifting economic arrangements.

Like the birth control statutes involved in *Griswold* and
Baird, the abortion statutes involved in *Roe v. Wade,* and
in the case before us today apply equally to decisions
made by married persons and by unmarried persons. . . .

[T]he basic question is whether the "abortion decision"
should be made by the individual or by the majority "in
the unrestrained imposition of its own, extraconstitutional
value preferences." . . .

I should think it obvious that the State's interest in the
protection of an embryo - even if that interest is defined
as "protecting those who will be citizens," - increases pro-
gressively and dramatically as the organism's capacity to
feel pain, to experience pleasure, to survive, and to react
to its surroundings increases day by day. The development of a fetus - and pregnancy itself - are not static conditions, and the assertion that the government's interest is
static simply ignores this reality.

Nor is it an answer to argue that life itself is not a static
condition, and that "there is no nonarbitrary line separating a fetus from a child, or indeed, an adult human being."
For, unless the religious view that a fetus is a "person" is

adopted . . . there is a fundamental and well-recognized difference between a fetus and a human being; indeed, if there is not such a difference, the permissibility of terminating the life of a fetus could scarcely be left to the will of the state legislatures. And if distinctions may be drawn between a fetus and a human being in terms of the state interest in their protection - even though the fetus represents one of "those who will be citizens" - it seems to me quite odd to argue that distinctions may not also be drawn between the state interest in protecting the freshly fertilized egg and the state interest in protecting the 9-month-gestated, fully sentient fetus on the eve of birth. Recognition of this distinction is supported not only by logic, but also by history and by our shared experiences.

. . . . [T]he fact that the doctrine of stare decisis [let past decisions stand] is not an absolute bar to the reexamination of past interpretations of the Constitution [does not] mean that the values underlying that doctrine may be summarily put to one side. There is a strong public interest in stability, and in the orderly conduct of our affairs, that is served by a consistent course of constitutional adjudication. Acceptance of the fundamental premises that underlie the decision in *Roe v. Wade*, as well as the application of those premises in that case, places the primary responsibility for decision in matters of childbearing squarely in the private sector of our society. The majority remains free to preach the evils of birth control and abortion and to persuade others to make correct decisions while the individual faced with the reality of a difficult choice having serious and personal consequences of major importance to her own future - perhaps to the salvation of her own immortal soul - remains free to seek and to obtain sympathetic guidance from those who share her own value preferences.

In the final analysis, the holding in *Roe v. Wade* presumes that it is far better to permit some individuals to make incorrect decisions than to deny all individuals the right to make decisions that have a profound effect upon their destiny. Arguably a very primitive society would have been protected from evil by a rule against eating apples; a majority familiar with Adam's experience might favor such a rule. But the lawmakers who placed a special premium on the protection of individual liberty have recognized that certain values are more important than the will of a transient majority.

CHIEF JUSTICE BURGER, dissenting: . . . . [E]very member of the *Roe* Court rejected the idea of abortion on demand. The Court's opinion today, however, plainly undermines that important principle, and I regretfully conclude that some of the concerns of the dissenting Justices in *Roe*, as well as the concerns I expressed in my separate opinion, have now been realized.

The extent to which the Court has departed from the limitations expressed in *Roe* is readily apparent. In *Roe*, the Court emphasized "that the State does have an important and legitimate interest in preserving and protecting the health of the pregnant woman. . . ."

Yet today the Court astonishingly goes so far as to say that the State may not even require that a woman contemplating an abortion be provided with accurate medical information concerning the risks inherent in the medical procedure which she is about to undergo and the availability of state-funded alternatives if she elects not to run those risks. Can anyone doubt that the State could impose a similar requirement with respect to other medical procedures? Can anyone doubt that doctors routinely give

similar information concerning risks in countless procedures having far less impact on life and health, both physical and emotional than an abortion, and risk a malprac-
tice lawsuit if they fail to do so?

Yet the Court concludes that the State cannot impose this
simple information-dispensing requirement in the abortion context where the decision is fraught with serious
physical, psychological, and moral concerns of the highest
order. Can it possibly be that the Court is saying that the
Constitution *forbids* the communication of such critical
information to a woman? We have apparently already
passed the point at which abortion is available merely on
demand. If the statute at issue here is to be invalidated,
the "demand" will not even have to be the result of an informed choice.

The Court in *Roe* further recognized that the State "has
still *another* important and legitimate interest" which is
"separate and distinct" from the interest in protecting maternal health, i.e., an interest in "protecting the potentiality of human life." The point at which these interests become "compelling" under *Roe* is at viability of the fetus.
Today, however, the Court abandons that standard and
renders the solemnly stated concerns of the 1973 *Roe*
opinion for the interests of the states mere shallow rhetoric. The statute at issue in this case requires that a second
physician be present during an abortion performed after
viability, so that the second physician can "take control of
the child and . . . provide immediate medical care . . . taking all reasonable steps necessary, in his judgment, to preserve the child's life and health."

Essentially this provision simply states that a viable fetus
is to be cared for, not destroyed. No governmental power

exists to say that a viable fetus should not have every protection required to preserve its life. Undoubtedly the
Pennsylvania Legislature added the second-physician requirement on the mistaken assumption that this Court
meant what it said in *Roe* concerning the "compelling interest" of the states in potential life after viability.

The Court's opinion today is but the most recent indication of the distance traveled since *Roe.* Perhaps the first
important road marker was the Court's holding in
Planned Parenthood of Central Missouri v. Danforth, in
which the Court held (over the dissent of Justice White
joined by Justice Rehnquist and myself) that the State
may not require that minors seeking an abortion first obtain parental consent. Parents, not judges or social work-
ers, have the inherent right and responsibility to advise
their children in matters of this sensitivity and consequence. Can one imagine a surgeon performing an ampu-
tation or even an appendectomy on a 14-year-old girl
without the consent of a parent or guardian except in an
emergency situation?

Yet today the Court goes beyond *Danforth* by remanding
[returning to the lower court] for further consideration of
the provisions of Pennsylvania's statute requiring that a
minor seeking an abortion without parental consent petition the appropriate court for authorization. Even if I
were to agree that the Constitution requires that the states
may not provide that a minor receive parental consent before undergoing an abortion, I would certainly hold that
judicial approval may be required. This is in keeping
with the longstanding common-law principle that courts
may function in loco parentis [in place of the parent]
when parents are unavailable or neglectful, even though
courts are not very satisfactory substitutes when the issue

is whether a 12-, 14-, or 16-year-old unmarried girl should
have an abortion. In my view, no remand is necessary on
this point because the statutory provision in question is
constitutional.

In discovering constitutional infirmities in state regulations of abortion that are in accord with our history and
tradition, we may have lured judges into "roaming at large
in the constitutional field." The soundness of our holdings must be tested by the decisions that purport to follow
them. If *Danforth* and today's holding really mean what
they seem to say, I agree we should reexamine *Roe*.

JUSTICE WHITE (joined by Justice Rehnquist), dissenting: Today the Court carries forward the "difficult and
continuing venture in substantive due process" that began
with the decision in *Roe v. Wade*, and has led the Court
further and further afield in the 13 years since that decision was handed down. I was in dissent in *Roe v. Wade*
and am in dissent today. . . . [I]n my view, our precedents
in this area, applied in a manner consistent with sound
principles of constitutional adjudication, require reversal
of the Court of Appeals on the ground that the provisions
before us are facially constitutional.

The rule of stare decisis [let past decisions stand] is essential if case-by-case judicial decision-making is to be recon-
ciled with the principle of the rule of law, for when governing legal standards are open to revision in every case,
deciding cases becomes a mere exercise of judicial will,
with arbitrary and unpredictable results. But stare decisis
is not the only constraint upon judicial decisionmaking.
Cases - like this one - that involve our assumed power to
set aside on grounds of unconstitutionality a state or federal statute representing the democratically expressed will

of the people call other considerations into play. Because the Constitution itself is ordained and established by the people of the United States, constitutional adjudication by this Court does not, in theory at any rate, frustrate the authority of the people to govern themselves through institutions of their own devising and in accordance with principles of their own choosing. But decisions that find in the Constitution principles or values that cannot fairly be read into that document usurp the people's authority, for such decisions represent choices that the people have never made and that they cannot disavow through corrective legislation. For this reason, it is essential that this Court maintain the power to restore authority to its proper possessors by correcting constitutional decisions that, on reconsideration, are found to be mistaken.

.... Stare decisis did not stand in the way of the Justices who, in the late 1930's, swept away constitutional doctrines that had placed unwarranted restrictions on the power of the State and Federal Governments to enact social and economic legislation. Nor did stare decisis deter a different set of Justices, some 15 years later, from rejecting the theretofore prevailing view that the Fourteenth Amendment permitted the States to maintain the system of racial segregation. In both instances, history has been far kinder to those who departed from precedent [a past decision binding on all future similar decisions] than to those who would have blindly followed the rule of stare decisis. ...

In my view, the time has come to recognize that *Roe v. Wade* ... "departs from a proper understanding" of the Constitution and to overrule it. ... That the flaws in an opinion were evident at the time it was handed down is hardly a reason for adhering to it.

Roe v. Wade posits that a woman has a fundamental right
to terminate her pregnancy, and that this right may be restricted only in the service of two compelling state interests: the interest in maternal health (which becomes compelling only at the stage in pregnancy at which an abortion becomes more hazardous than carrying the pregnancy
to term) and the interest in protecting the life of the fetus
(which becomes compelling only at the point of viability).
A reader of the Constitution might be surprised to find
that it encompassed these detailed rules, for the text obviously contains no references to abortion, nor, indeed, to
pregnancy or reproduction generally; and, of course, it is
highly doubtful that the authors of any of the provisions
of the Constitution believed that they were giving protection to abortion. As its prior cases clearly show, however,
this Court does not subscribe to the simplistic view that
constitutional interpretation can possibly be limited to the
"plain meaning" of the Constitution's text or to the sub-
jective intention of the Framers. The Constitution is not
a deed setting forth the precise metes and bounds of its
subject matter; rather, it is a document announcing fundamental principles in value-laden terms that leave ample
scope for the exercise of normative judgment by those
charged with interpreting and applying it. In particular,
the Due Process Clause of the Fourteenth Amendment,
which forbids the deprivation of "life, liberty, or property
without due process of law," has been read by the majority of the Court to be broad enough to provide substantive
protection against state infringement of a broad range of
individual interests.

In most instances, the substantive protection afforded the
liberty or property of an individual by the Fourteenth
Amendment is extremely limited: State action impinging
on individual interests need only be rational to survive

scrutiny under the Due Process Clause, and the determination of rationality is to be made with a heavy dose of deference to the policy choices of the legislature. Only "fundamental" rights are entitled to the added protection provided by strict judicial scrutiny of legislation that impinges upon them. I can certainly agree with the proposition - which I deem indisputable - that a woman's ability to choose an abortion is a species of "liberty" that is subject to the general protections of the Due Process Clause. I cannot agree, however, that this liberty is so "fundamental" that restrictions upon it call into play anything more than the most minimal judicial scrutiny.

Fundamental liberties and interests are more clearly present when the Constitution provides specific textual recognition of their existence and importance. Thus, the Court is on relatively firm ground when it deems certain of the liberties set forth in the Bill of Rights to be fundamental and therefore finds them incorporated in the Fourteenth Amendment's guarantee that no State may deprive any person of liberty without due process of law. When the Court ventures further and defines as "fundamental" liberties that are nowhere mentioned in the Constitution (or that are present only in the so-called "penumbras" of specifically enumerated rights), it must, of necessity, act with more caution, lest it open itself to the accusation that, in the name of identifying constitutional principles to which the people have consented in framing their Constitution, the Court has done nothing more than impose its own controversial choices of value upon the people.

.... The Court has justified the recognition of a woman's fundamental right to terminate her pregnancy by invoking decisions upholding claims of personal autonomy in connection with the conduct of family life, the rearing of children, marital privacy, and the use of contraceptives, and the preservation of the individual's capacity to procreate. Even if each of these cases was correctly decided and could be properly grounded in rights that are "implicit in the concept of ordered liberty" or "deeply rooted in this Nation's history and tradition," the issues in the cases cited differ from those at stake where abortion is concerned. As the Court appropriately recognized in *Roe v. Wade*, "[t]he pregnant woman cannot be isolated in her privacy," the termination of a pregnancy typically involves the destruction of another entity: the fetus. However one answers the metaphysical or theological question whether the fetus is a "human being" or the legal question whether it is a "person" as that term is used in the Constitution, one must at least recognize, first, that the fetus is an entity that bears in its cells all the genetic information that characterizes a member of the species homo sapiens and distinguishes an individual member of that special from all others, and second, that there is no nonarbitrary line separating a fetus from a child or, indeed, an adult human being. Given that the continued existence and development - that is to say, the *life* - of such an entity are so directly at stake in the woman's decision whether or not to terminate her pregnancy, that decision must be recognized as . . . different in kind from the others that the Court has protected under the rubric of personal or family privacy and autonomy. Accordingly, the decisions cited by the Court both in *Roe* and in its opinion today as precedent for the fundamental nature of the liberty to choose abortion do not, even if all are accepted as valid, dictate the Court's classification.

If the woman's liberty to choose an abortion is fundamental, then, it is not because any of our precedents (aside from *Roe* itself) command or justify that result; it can only be because protection for this unique choice is itself "implicit in the concept of ordered liberty" or, perhaps, "deeply rooted in this Nation's history and tradition." It seems clear to me that it is neither. The Court's opinion in *Roe* itself convincingly refutes the notion that the abortion liberty is deeply rooted in the history or tradition of our people, as does the continuing and deep division of the people themselves over the question of abortion. As for the notion that choice in the matter of abortion is implicit in the concept of ordered liberty, it seems apparent to me that a free, egalitarian, and democratic society does not presuppose any particular rule or set of rules with respect to abortion. And again, the fact that many men and women of good will and high commitment to constitutional government place themselves on both sides of the abortion controversy strengthens my own conviction that the values animating the Constitution do not compel recognition of the abortion liberty as fundamental. In so denominating that liberty, the Court engages not in constitutional interpretation, but in the unrestrained imposition of its own, extraconstitutional value preferences.

A second, equally basic error infects the Court's decision in *Roe v. Wade.* The detailed set of rules governing state restrictions on abortion that the Court first articulated in *Roe* and has since refined and elaborated presupposes not only that the woman's liberty to choose an abortion is fundamental, but also that the State's countervailing interest in protecting fetal life (or, as the Court would have it, "potential human life" becomes "compelling" only at the point at which the fetus is viable. . . . [T]he Court's choice of viability as the point at which the State's interest becomes compelling is entirely arbitrary. . . .

The governmental interest at issue is in protecting those who will be citizens if their lives are not ended in the womb. The substantiality of this interest is in no way dependent on the probability that the fetus may be capable of surviving outside the womb at any given point in its development. . . . The State's interest is in the fetus as an entity in itself, and the character of this entity does not change at the point of viability under conventional medical wisdom. Accordingly, the State's interest, if compelling after viability, is equally compelling before viability.

Both the characterization of the abortion liberty as fundamental and the denigration of the State's interest in preserving the lives of nonviable fetuses are essential to the detailed set of constitutional rules devised by the Court to limit the States' power to regulate abortion. If either or both of these facets of *Roe v. Wade* were rejected, a broad range of limitations on abortion (including outright prohibition) that are now unavailable to the States would again become constitutional possibilities.

In my view, such a state of affairs would be highly desirable from the standpoint of the Constitution. Abortion is a hotly contested moral and political issue. Such issues, in our society, are to be resolved by the will of the people, either as expressed through legislation or through the general principles they have already incorporated into the Constitution they have adopted. *Roe v. Wade* implies that the people have already resolved the debate by weaving into the Constitution the values and principles that answer the issue. As I have argued, I believe it is clear that the people have never - not in 1787, 1791, 1868, or at any time since - done any such thing. I would return the issue to the people by overruling *Roe v. Wade.*

As it has evolved in the decisions of this Court, the freedom recognized by the Court in *Roe v. Wade* and its progeny is essentially a negative one, based not on the notion that abortion is a good in itself, but only on the view that the legitimate goals that may be served by state coercion of private choices regarding abortion are, at least under some circumstances, outweighed by the damage to individual autonomy and privacy that such coercion entails. In other words, the evil of abortion does not justify the evil of forbidding it. But precisely because *Roe v. Wade* is not premised on the notion that abortion is itself desirable (either as a matter of constitutional entitlement or of social policy), the decision does not command the States to fund or encourage abortion, or even to approve of it. Rather, we have recognized that the States may legitimately adopt a policy of encouraging normal childbirth rather than abortion so long as the measures through which that policy is implemented do not amount to direct compulsion of the woman's choice regarding abortion. The provisions before the Court today quite obviously represent the State's effort to implement such a policy.

. . . . The majority . . . seems to find it necessary to respond by changing the rules to invalidate what before would have seemed permissible. The result is a decision that finds no justification in the Court's previous holdings, departs from sound principles of constitutional and statutory interpretation, and unduly limits the State's power to implement the legitimate (and in some circumstances compelling) policy of encouraging normal childbirth in preference to abortion.

The Court begins by striking down statutory provisions designed to ensure that the woman's choice of an abortion is fully informed - that is, that she is aware not only of the reasons for having an abortion, but also of the risks associated with an abortion and the availability of assistance that might make the alternative of normal childbirth more attractive than it might otherwise appear. . . .

One searches the majority's opinion in vain for a convincing reason why the apparently laudable policy of promoting informed consent becomes unconstitutional when the subject is abortion. . . . As the majority concedes, the statute does not, on its face, require that the patient be given any information that is false or unverifiable. Moreover, it is unquestionable that all of the information required would be relevant in many cases to a woman's decision whether or not to obtain an abortion.

. . . . I fail to see how providing a woman with accurate information - whether relevant or irrelevant - could ever be deemed to impair *any* constitutionally protected interest (even if, as the majority hypothesizes, the information may upset her). Thus, the majority's observation that the statute may require the provision of irrelevant information in some cases is itself an irrelevancy.

. . . . It is in the very nature of informed-consent provisions that they may produce some anxiety in the patient and influence her in her choice. This is in fact their reason for existence, and - provided that the information required is accurate and nonmisleading - it is an entirely salutary reason. If information may reasonably affect the patient's choice, the patient should have that information; and, as one authority has observed, "the greater the likelihood that particular information will influence [the patient's] decision, the more essential the information arguably becomes for securing her informed consent." That the result of the provision of information may be that some women will forgo abortions by no means suggests that providing the information is unconstitutional, for the ostensible objective of *Roe v. Wade* is not maximizing the number of abortions, but maximizing choice. Moreover, our decisions in *Maher, Beal*, and *Harris v. McRae* all indicate that the State may encourage women to make their choice in favor of childbirth rather than abortion, and the provision of accurate information regarding abortion and its alternatives is a reasonable and fair means of achieving that objective.

. . . . I can concede that the Constitution extends its protection to certain zones of personal autonomy and privacy, and I can understand, if not share, the notion that the protection may extend to a woman's decision regarding abortion. But I cannot concede the possibility that the Constitution provides more than minimal protection for the manner in which a physician practices his or her profession or for the "dialogues" in which he or she chooses to participate in the course of treating patients. I had thought it clear that regulation of the practice of medicine, like regulation of other professions and of economic affairs generally, was a matter peculiarly within the competence of legislatures, and that such regulation was subject to review only for rationality.

. . . . [I]f the State may not "structure" the dialogue between doctor and patient, it should also follow that the State may not, for example, require attorneys to disclose to their clients information concerning the risks of representing the client in a particular proceeding. . . .

The rationale for state efforts to regulate the practice of a profession or vocation is simple: the government is entitled not to trust members of a profession to police themselves, and accordingly the legislature may for the most part impose such restrictions on the practice of a profession or business as it may find necessary to the protection of the public. This is precisely the rationale for infringing the professional freedom of doctors by imposing disclosure requirements upon them.... Unless one is willing to recast entirely the law with respect to the legitimacy of state regulation of professional conduct, the obvious rationality of the policy of promoting informed patient choice on the subject of abortion must defeat any claim that the disclosure requirements imposed by Pennsylvania are invalid because they infringe on "professional freedom" or on the "physician-patient relationship."

.... [B]ecause the informed-consent provisions do not infringe the essential right at issue - the right of the woman to choose to have an abortion - the majority's conclusion that the provisions are unconstitutional is without foundation.

The majority's decision to strike down the reporting requirements of the statute is equally extraordinary. The requirements obviously serve legitimate purposes. The information contained in the reports is highly relevant to the State's efforts to enforce Section 3210(a) of the statute, which forbids abortion of viable fetuses except when necessary to the mother's health. The information concerning complications plainly serves the legitimate goal of advancing the state of medical knowledge concerning maternal and fetal health. Given that the subject of abortion is a matter of considerable public interest and debate (constrained to some extent, of course, by the pre-emptive effect of this Court's ill-conceived constitutional decisions), the collection and dissemination of demographic information concerning abortions is clearly a legitimate goal of public policy. Moreover, there is little reason to believe that the required reports, though fairly detailed, would impose an undue burden on physicians and impede the ability of their patients to obtain abortions, as all of the information required would necessarily be readily available to a physician who had performed an abortion. Accordingly, under this Court's prior decisions in this area, the reporting requirements are constitutional.

.... I can accept the proposition that a statute whose purpose and effect are to allow harassment and intimidation of citizens for their constitutionally protected conduct is unconstitutional, but the majority's action in striking down the Pennsylvania statute on this basis is . . . indefensible. . . .

The information contained in the reports identifies the patient on the basis of age, race, marital status, and "political subdivision" of residence; the remainder of the information included in the reports concerns the medical aspects of the abortion. It is implausible that a particular patient could be identified on the basis of the combination of the general identifying information and the specific medical information in these reports by anyone who did not already know (at a minimum) that the woman had been pregnant and obtained an abortion. Accordingly, the provisions pose little or no threat to the woman's privacy.

In sum, there is no basis here even for a preliminary injunction [court order to stop an action] against the reporting provisions of the statute, much less for a final determination that the provisions are unconstitutional.

The majority resorts to linguistic nit-picking in striking down the provision requiring physicians aborting viable fetuses to use the method of abortion most likely to result in fetal survival unless that method would pose a "significantly greater medical risk to the life or health of the pregnant woman" than would other available methods. The majority concludes that the statute's use of the word "significantly" indicates that the statute represents an unlawful "trade-off" between the woman's health and the chance of fetal survival. Not only is this conclusion based on a wholly unreasonable interpretation of the statute, but the statute would also be constitutional even if it meant what the majority says it means.

.... [I]f the State's interest in preserving the life of a viable fetus is, as *Roe* purported to recognize, a compelling one, the State is at the very least entitled to demand that that interest not be subordinated to a purported maternal health risk that is in fact wholly insubstantial. The statute, on its face, demands no more than this of a doctor performing an abortion of a viable fetus.

Even if the Pennsylvania statute is properly interpreted as requiring a pregnant woman seeking abortion of a viable fetus to endure a method of abortion chosen to protect the health of the fetus despite the existence of an alternative that in some substantial degree is more protective of her own health, I am not convinced that the statute is unconstitutional. ...

The Court's ruling in this respect is not even *consistent* with its decision in *Roe v. Wade.* In *Roe*, the Court conceded that the State's interest in preserving the life of a viable fetus is a compelling one, and the Court has never disavowed that concession. The Court now holds that this compelling interest cannot justify *any* regulation that imposes a quantifiable medical risk upon the pregnant woman who seeks to abort a viable fetus: if attempting to save the fetus imposes any additional risk of injury to the woman, she must be permitted to kill it. This holding hardly accords with the usual understanding of the term "compelling interest," which we have used to describe those governmental interests that are so weighty as to justify substantial and ordinarily impermissible impositions on the individual - impositions that, I had thought, could include the infliction of some degree of risk of physical harm. . . . I find the majority's unwillingness to tolerate the imposition of *any* nonnegligible risk of injury to a pregnant woman in order to protect the life of her viable fetus in the course of an abortion baffling.

The Court's ruling today that any trade-off between the woman's health and fetal survival is impermissible is not only inconsistent with *Roe's* recognition of a compelling state interest in viable fetal life; it directly contradicts one of the essential holdings of *Roe* - that is, that the State may forbid *all* postviability abortions except when *necessary* to protect the life or health of the pregnant woman. . . . Pennsylvania . . . has simply required that when an abortion of some kind is medically necessary, it shall be conducted so as to spare the fetus (to the greatest degree possible) unless a method less protective of the fetus is itself to some degree medically necessary for the woman. . . . [F]or some reason, the Court concludes that whereas the trade-offs it devises are compelled by the Constitution, the essentially indistinguishable trade-off the State has attempted is foreclosed. This cannot be the law.

The framework of rights and interests devised by the Court in *Roe v. Wade* indicates that just as a State may prohibit a postviability abortion unless it is necessary to protect the life or health of the woman, the State may require that postviability abortions be conducted using the method most protective of the fetus unless a less protective method is necessary to protect the life or health of the woman. Under this standard, the Pennsylvania statute - which does not require the woman to accept any significant health risks to protect the fetus - is plainly constitutional.

The Court strikes down the statute's second-physician requirement because, in its view, the existence of a medical emergency requiring an immediate abortion to save the life of the pregnant woman would not be a defense to a prosecution under the statute. The Court does not question the proposition, established in the *Ashcroft* case, that a second-physician requirement accompanied by an exception for emergencies is a permissible means of vindicating the compelling state interest in protecting the lives of viable fetuses. Accordingly, the majority's ruling on this issue does not on its face involve a substantial departure from the Court's previous decisions.

. . . . [A] defense of medical necessity is fully as protective of the interests of the pregnant woman as a defense of "emergency." The Court falls back on the notion that the legislature "knows how to provide a medical-emergency exception when it chooses to do so." No doubt. But the legislature obviously also "knows how" to provide a medical-necessity exception, and it has done so. Why this exception is insufficient is unexplained and inexplicable.

The Court's rejection of a perfectly plausible reading of the statute flies in the face of the principle - which until today I had thought applicable to abortion statutes as well as to other legislative enactments - that "[w]here fairly possible, courts should construe a statute to avoid a danger of unconstitutionality." The Court's reading is obviously based on an entirely different principle: that in cases involving abortion, a permissible reading of a statute is to be avoided at all costs. Not sharing this viewpoint, I cannot accept the majority's conclusion that the statute does not provide for the equivalent of a defense of emergency.

. . . . The decision today appears symptomatic of the Court's own insecurity over its handiwork in *Roe v. Wade* and the cases following that decision. Aware that in *Roe* it essentially created something out of nothing and that there are many in this country who hold that decision to be basically illegitimate, the Court responds defensively. Perceiving, in a statute implementing the State's legitimate policy of preferring childbirth to abortion, a threat to or criticism of the decision in *Roe v. Wade*, the majority indiscriminately strikes down statutory provisions that in no way contravene the right recognized in *Roe*. I do not share the warped point of view of the majority, nor can I follow the tortuous path the majority treads in proceeding to strike down the statute before us. I dissent.

JUSTICE O'CONNOR (joined by Justice Rehnquist), dissenting: This Court's abortion decisions have already worked a major distortion in the Court's constitutional jurisprudence. Today's decision goes further, and makes it painfully clear that no legal rule or doctrine is safe from . . . nullification by this Court when an occasion for its application arises in a case involving state regulation of abortion. The permissible scope of abortion regulation is not the only constitutional issue on which this Court is divided, but - except when it comes to abortion - the Court has generally refused to let such disagreements, however longstanding or deeply felt, prevent it from evenhandedly applying uncontroversial legal doctrines to cases that come before it. That the Court's unworkable scheme for constitutionalizing the regulation of abortion has had this institutionally debilitating effect should not be surprising, however, since the Court is not suited to the expansive role it has claimed for itself in the series of cases that began with *Roe v. Wade*. . . .

I believe the proper course is to decide this case as the Court of Appeals should have decided it, lest [American College] suffer the very prejudice the Court sees fit to inflict on [Thornburgh]. For me, then, the question is not one of "success" but of the "likelihood of success." In addition, because Pennsylvania has not asked the Court to reconsider or overrule *Roe v. Wade*, I do not address that question.

I do, however, remain of the views expressed in my dissent in *Akron*. The State has compelling interests in ensuring maternal health and in protecting potential human life, and these interests exist "throughout pregnancy." Under this Court's fundamental-rights jurisprudence, judicial scrutiny of state regulation of abortion should be limited to whether the state law bears a rational relationship to legitimate purposes such as the advancement of these compelling interests, with heightened scrutiny reserved for instances in which the State has imposed an "undue burden" on the abortion decision. An undue burden will generally be found "in situations involving absolute obstacles or severe limitations on the abortion decision," not wherever a state regulation "may 'inhibit' abortions to some degree.

And if a state law does interfere with the abortion decision to an extent that is unduly burdensome, so that it becomes "necessary to apply an exacting standard of
review," the possibility remains that the statute will with-
stand the stricter scrutiny.

These principles for evaluating state regulation of abortion were not newly minted in my dissenting opinion in
Akron. Apart from *Roe*'s outmoded trimester framework,
the "unduly burdensome" standard had been articulated
and applied with fair consistency by this Court in cases
such as *Harris v. McRae, Maher v. Roe, Beal v. Doe,* and
Belotti v. Baird. In *Akron* and *Ashcroft* the Court, in my
view, distorted and misapplied this standard, but made no
clean break with precedent and indeed "follow[ed] this
approach" in assessing some of the regulations before it in
those cases.

The Court today goes well beyond mere distortion of the
"unduly burdensome" standard. By holding that each of
the challenged provisions is facially unconstitutional as a
matter of law, and that no conceivable facts [Thornburgh]
might offer could alter this result, the Court appears to
adopt as its new test a per se rule under which any regulation touching on abortion must be invalidated if it poses
"an unacceptable danger of deterring the exercise of that
right." Under this prophylactic test, it seems that the
mere possibility that some women will be less likely to
choose to have an abortion by virtue of the presence of a
particular state regulation suffices to invalidate it. Simul-
taneously, the Court strains to discover "the anti-abortion
character of the statute," and . . . invents an unprecedented
canon of construction under which "in cases involving
abortion, a permissible reading of a statute is to be avoid-

ed at all costs." I shall not belabor the dangerous extravagance of this dual approach, because I hope it represents merely a temporary aberration rather than a portent of lasting change in settled principles of constitutional law. Suffice it to say that I dispute not only the wisdom but also the legitimacy of the Court's attempt to discredit and pre-empt state abortion regulation regardless of the interests it serves and the impact it has.

Under the "unduly burdensome" test, the District Judge's conclusion that [American College was] not entitled to a preliminary injunction [court order stopping an action] was clearly correct. Indeed, the District Judge applied essentially that test, after suggesting that no "meaningful distinction can be made between . . . 'legally significant burden' and . . . 'undue burden.'" I begin, as does the Court, with the Act's informed consent provisions.

The Court condemns some specific features of the informed consent provisions of Section 3205, and issues a blanket condemnation of the provisions in their entirety as irrelevant or distressing in some cases and as intruding on the relationship between the woman and her physician. . . . The "parade of horribles" the Court invalidated in *Akron* is missing here. For example, Section 3205(a)(iii) requires that the woman be informed, "when medically accurate", of the risks associated with a particular abortion procedure, and Section 3205(a)(v) requires the physician to inform the woman of "[t]he medical risks associated with carrying her child to term." This is the kind of balanced information I would have thought all could agree is relevant to a woman's informed consent.

I do not dismiss the possibility that requiring the physician or counselor to read aloud the State's printed materials if the woman wishes access to them but cannot read raises First Amendment concerns. Even the requirement that women who can read be informed of the availability of those materials, and furnished with them on request, may create some possibility that the physician or counselor is being required to "communicate [the State's] ideology." . . .

The Court singles out for specific criticism the required description, in the printed materials, of fetal characteristics at 2-week intervals. These materials, of course, will be shown to the woman only if she chooses to inspect them. If the materials were sufficiently inflammatory and inaccurate the fact that the woman must ask to see them would not necessarily preclude finding an undue burden, but there is no indication that this is true of the description of fetal characteristics the statute contemplates. . . . [T]he information is certainly rationally related to the State's interests in ensuring informed consent and in protecting potential human life. Similarly, . . . [in] Section 3205's requirements that the woman be informed of the availability of medical assistance benefits and of the father's legal responsibility[, the] information is indisputably relevant in many cases and would not appear to place a severe limitation on the abortion decision.

The Court's rationale for striking down the reporting requirements of Section 3214 . . . rests on an unsupported finding of fact by this Court to the effect that "[i]dentification is the obvious purpose of these extreme reporting requirements." . . . I do not . . . see a substantial threat of identification on the face of the statute, which does not require disclosure of the woman's identity to anyone, and which provides that reports shall be disclosed to the public only in "a form which will not lead to the disclosure of the identity of any person filing a report." I therefore conclude that the District Judge correctly ruled that [American College is] unlikely to succeed in establishing an undue burden on the abortion decision stemming from the possibility of identification.

. . . . Since Section 3210(b) can fairly be read to require "only that the risk be a real and identifiable one," there is little possibility that a woman's abortion decision will be unduly burdened by risks falling below that threshold. Accordingly, Section 3210(b) should not be preliminarily enjoined, and I express no opinion as to the point at which a "trade-off" between the health of the woman and the survival of the fetus would rise to the level of an undue burden.

. . . . [T]his provision is constitutional under *Ashcroft* because the Act effectively provides for an exception making this requirement inapplicable in emergency situations. . . . [T]he preliminary injunction entered against enforcement of the Act's parental notice and consent provisions should be vacated [annulled], since, as in *Ashcroft*, there is no reason here to believe that the State will not provide for the expedited procedures called for by its statute. . . .

In my view, today's decision makes bad constitutional law and bad procedural law. The "'undesired and uncomfortable straitjacket'" in this case is not the one the Court purports to discover in Pennsylvania's statute; it is the one the Court has tailored for the 50 States. I respectfully dissent.

WEBSTER v.
REPRODUCTIVE HEALTH SERVICES

EXCERPTS

"Missouri's refusal to allow public employees to perform abortions in public hospitals leaves a pregnant woman with the same choices as if the State had chosen not to operate any public hospitals at all."

Justice William Rehnquist

"For today, at least, the law of abortion stands undisturbed. For today, the women of this Nation still retain the liberty to control their destinies. But the signs are evident and very ominous, and a chill wind blows."

Justice Harry Blackmun

In Brief

Question: Are the Missouri abortion laws constitutional?

Lower Court: U.S. District Court, Western Missouri
                U.S. Court of Appeals, Eighth Circuit

Law: Missouri Abortion Act (1986)

Parties: William Webster, Missouri Attorney General
            Reproductive Health Services

Counsel: For Webster: William Webster
            For RHS: Frank Susman

Arguments: April 26, 1989

Decision: July 3, 1989

Majority: Chief Justice Rehnquist, Justices White,
            O'Connor, Scalia, Kennedy

Minority: Justices Brennan, Marshall, Blackmun, Stevens

Decision by: Justice Rehnquist (p. 180)

Concurrences: Justice O'Connor (p. 193
               Justice Scalia (p. 198)

Concurrences in part/Dissents in part:

            Justice Blackmun (p. 201)
            Justice Stevens (p. 215)

Offical Text: U.S. Reports, Vol. 492, p. 490
Lower Court: Federal Supplement, Vol. 662, p. 407
              Federal Reporter 2d, Vol. 851, p. 1071

THE WEBSTER COURT

Chief Justice William Rehnquist
Appointed Associate Justice 1971 by Richard M. Nixon
Appointed Chief Justice 1986 by Ronald W. Reagan

Associate Justice William Brennan
Appointed 1956 by Dwight D. Eisenhower

Associate Justice Byron White
Appointed 1962 by John F. Kennedy

Associate Justice Thurgood Marshall
Appointed 1967 by Lyndon B. Johnson

Associate Justice Harry Blackmun
Appointed 1970 by Richard M. Nixon

Associate Justice John Paul Stevens
Appointed 1975 by Gerald R. Ford

Associate Justice Sandra Day O'Connor
Appointed 1981 by Ronald W. Reagan

Associate Justice Antonin Scalia
Appointed 1986 by Ronald W. Reagan

Associate Justice Anthony Kennedy
Appointed 1988 by Ronald W. Reagan

WEBSTER v. REPRODUCTIVE HEALTH SERVICES

July 3, 1989

CHIEF JUSTICE WILLIAM REHNQUIST announced the judgment of the Court: This appeal concerns the constitutionality of a Missouri statute regulating the performance of abortions. The United States Court of Appeals for the Eighth Circuit struck down several provisions of the statute on the ground that they violated this Court's decision in *Roe v. Wade* and cases following it. We . . . now reverse.

In June 1986, the Governor of Missouri signed into law Missouri Senate Committee Substitute for House Bill No. 1596 (hereinafter Act or statute), which amended existing state law concerning unborn children and abortions. The Act consisted of 20 provisions, 5 of which are now before the Court. The first provision, or preamble, contains "findings" by the state legislature that "[t]he life of each human being begins at conception," and that "unborn children have protectable interests in life, health, and well-being." The Act further requires that all Missouri laws be interpreted to provide unborn children with the same rights enjoyed by other persons, subject to the Federal Constitution and this Court's precedents. Among its other provisions, the Act requires that, prior to performing an abortion on any woman whom a physician has reason to believe is 20 or more weeks pregnant, the physician ascertain whether the fetus is viable by performing "such medical examinations and tests as are necessary to make a finding of the gestational age, weight, and lung maturity

of the unborn child." The Act also prohibits the use of
public employees and facilities to perform or assist abortions not necessary to save the mother's life, and it prohibits the use of public funds, employees, or facilities for
the purpose of "encouraging or counseling" a woman to
have an abortion not necessary to save her life.

In July 1986, five health professionals employed by the
State and two nonprofit corporations brought this class action [suit by a group with similarities] in the United
States District Court . . . to challenge the constitutionality
of the Missouri statute. . . . [and] sought . . . relief on the
ground that certain statutory provisions violated the First,
Fourth, Ninth, and Fourteenth Amendments to the Federal Constitution. They asserted violations of various rights,
including the "privacy rights of pregnant women seeking
abortions"; the "woman's right to an abortion"; the
"righ[t] to privacy in the physician-patient relationship";
the physician's "righ[t] to practice medicine"; the pregnant woman's "right to life due to inherent risks involved
in childbirth"; and the woman's right to "receive . . . adequate medical advice and treatment" concerning abortions.

. . . . The two nonprofit corporations are Reproductive
Health Services, which offers family planning and gyneco-
logical services to the public, including abortion services
up to 22 weeks "gestational age," and Planned Parenthood
of Kansas City, which provides abortion services up to 14
weeks gestational age. The individual[s] are three physicians, one nurse, and a social worker. All are "public employees" at "public facilities" in Missouri, and they are
paid for their services with "public funds." The individual[s], within the scope of their public employment, encourage and counsel pregnant women to have nonthera-

peutic abortions. Two of the physicians perform abortions.

Several weeks after the complaint was filed, the District Court temporarily restrained enforcement of several provisions of the Act. Following a 3-day trial in December 1986, the District Court declared seven provisions of the Act unconstitutional and enjoined their enforcement. These provisions included the preamble, the "informed consent" provision, which required physicians to inform the pregnant woman of certain facts before performing an abortion; the requirement that post-16-week abortions be performed only in hospitals; the mandated tests to determine viability; and the prohibition on the use of public funds, employees, and facilities to perform or assist nontherapeutic abortions, and the restrictions on the use of public funds,, employees, and facilities to encourage or counsel women to have such abortions.

The Court of Appeals for the Eighth Circuit affirmed [confirmed]. . . .

Decision of this case requires us to address four sections of the Missouri Act: (a) the preamble; (b) the prohibition on the use of public facilities or employees to perform abortions; (c) the prohibition on public funding of abortion counseling; and (d) the requirement that physicians conduct viability tests prior to performing abortions. . . .

The Act's preamble, as noted, sets forth "findings" by the Missouri legislature that "[t]he life of each human being begins at conception," and that "[u]nborn children have protectable interests in life, health, and well-being." The

Act then mandates that state laws be interpreted to provide unborn children with "all the rights, privileges, and immunities available to other persons, citizens, and residents of this state," subject to the Constitution and this Court's precedents. . . .

Certainly the preamble does not by its terms regulate abortion or any other aspect of [Reproductive Health Services'] medical practice. The Court has emphasized that *Roe v. Wade* "implies no limitation on the authority of a State to make a value judgment favoring childbirth over abortion." The preamble can be read simply to express that sort of value judgment.

We think the extent to which the preamble's language might be used to interpret other state statutes or regulations is something that only the courts of Missouri can definitively decide. State law has offered protections to unborn children in tort and probate law, and Section 1.205.2 can be interpreted to do no more than that. . . .

It will be time enough for federal courts to address the meaning of the preamble should it be applied to restrict the activities of [Reproductive Health Services] in some concrete way. Until then, this Court "is not empowered to decide . . . abstract propositions, or to declare . . . principles or rules of law which cannot affect the result as to the thing in issue in the case before it." We therefore need not pass on the constitutionality of the Act's preamble.

Section 188.210 provides that "[i]t shall be unlawful for any public employee within the scope of his employment to perform or assist an abortion, not necessary to save the life of the mother," while Section 188.215 makes it "unlawful for any public facility to be used for the purpose of performing or assisting an abortion not necessary to save the life of the mother." The Court of Appeals held that these provisions contravened this Court's abortion decisions. We take the contrary view.

As we said earlier this Term in *DeShaney v. Winnebago County Dept. of Social Services*, "our cases have recognized that the Due Process Clauses generally confer no affirmative right to governmental aid, even where such aid may be necessary to secure life, liberty, or property interests of which the government itself may not deprive the individual." In *Maher v. Roe*, the Court upheld a Connecticut welfare regulation under which Medicaid recipients received payments for medical services related to childbirth, but not for nontherapeutic abortions. The Court rejected the claim that this unequal subsidization of childbirth and abortion was impermissible under *Roe v. Wade*. . . .

Relying on *Maher*, the Court in *Poelker v. Doe* held that the city of St. Louis committed "no constitutional violation . . . in electing, as a policy choice, to provide publicly financed hospital services for childbirth without providing corresponding services for nontherapeutic abortions."

More recently, in *Harris v. McRae*, the Court upheld "the most restrictive version of the Hyde Amendment," which withheld from States federal funds under the Medicaid program to reimburse the costs of abortions, "'except where the life of the mother would be endangered if the fetus were carried to term.'" As in *Maher* and *Poelker*, the Court required only a showing that Congress' authorization of "reimbursement for medically necessary services generally, but not for certain medically necessary abortions" was rationally related to the legitimate governmental goal of encouraging childbirth.

The Court of Appeals distinguished [explained the difference between cases] these cases on the ground that "[t]o prevent access to a public facility does more than demonstrate a political choice in favor of childbirth; it clearly narrows and in some cases forecloses the availability of abortion to women." The court reasoned that the ban on the use of public facilities "could prevent a woman's chosen doctor from performing an abortion because of his unprivileged status at other hospitals or because a private hospital adopted a similar anti-abortion stance." It also thought that "[s]uch a rule could increase the cost of obtaining an abortion and delay the timing of it as well."

We think that this analysis is much like that which we rejected in *Maher, Poelker,* and *McRae.* As in those cases, the State's decisions here to use public facilities and staff to encourage childbirth over abortion "places no governmental obstacle in the path of a woman who chooses to terminate her pregnancy." Just as Congress' refusal to fund abortions in *McRae* left "an indigent woman with at least the same range of choice in deciding whether to obtain a medically necessary abortion as she would have had if Congress had chosen to subsidize no health care costs at all," Missouri's refusal to allow public employees to perform abortions in public hospitals leaves a pregnant woman with the same choices as if the State had chosen not to operate any public hospitals at all. The challenged provisions only restrict a woman's ability to obtain an abortion to the extent that she chooses to use a physician affiliated with a public hospital. This circumstance is more easily remedied, and thus considerably less burdensome, than indigency, which "may make it difficult - and in some cases, perhaps, impossible - for some women to have abortions" without public funding. Having held that the State's refusal to fund abortions does not violate *Roe v. Wade*, it strains logic to reach a contrary result for the use of public facilities and employees. If the State may "make a value judgment favoring childbirth over abortion and . . . implement that judgment by the allocation of public funds," surely it may do so through the allocation of other public resources, such as hospitals and medical staff.

The Court of Appeals sought to distinguish our cases on the additional ground that "[t]he evidence here showed that all of the public facility's costs in providing abortion services are recouped when the patient pays." Absent any expenditure of public funds, the court thought that Missouri was "expressing" more than "its preference for childbirth over abortions," but rather was creating an "obstacle to exercise of the right to choose an abortion [that could not] stand absent a compelling state interest." We disagree.

"Constitutional concerns are greatest," we said in *Maher*, "when the State attempts to impose its will by the force of law; the State's power to encourage actions deemed to be in the public interest is necessarily far broader." Nothing in the Constitution requires States to enter or remain in the business of performing abortions. Nor . . . do private physicians and their patients have some kind of constitutional right of access to public facilities for the performance of abortions. Indeed, if the State does recoup all of its costs in performing abortions, and no state subsidy, direct or indirect, is available, it is difficult to see how any procreational choice is burdened by the State's ban on the use of its facilities or employees for performing abortions.

Maher, *Poelker*, and *McRae* all support the view that the State need not commit any resources to facilitating abortions, even if it can turn a profit by doing so. In *Poelker*, the suit was filed by an indigent who could not afford to pay for an abortion, but the ban on the performance of nontherapeutic abortions in city-owned hospitals applied whether or not the pregnant woman could pay. The Court emphasized that the Mayor's decision to prohibit abortions in city hospitals was "subject to public debate and approval or disapproval at the polls," and that "the Constitution does not forbid a State or city, pursuant to democratic processes, from expressing a preference for normal childbirth as St. Louis has done." Thus we uphold the Act's restrictions on the use of public employees and facilities for the performance or assistance of nontherapeutic abortions.

The Missouri Act contains three provisions relating to "encouraging or counseling a woman to have an abortion not necessary to save her life." Section 188.205 states that no public funds can be used for this purpose; Section 188.210 states that public employees cannot, within the scope of their employment, engage in such speech; and Section 188.215 forbids such speech in public facilities. The Court of Appeals . . . held that all three of these provisions were unconstitutionally vague, and that "the ban on using public funds, employees, and facilities to encourage or counsel a woman to have an abortion is an unacceptable infringement of the woman's fourteenth amendment right to choose an abortion after receiving the medical information necessary to exercise the right knowingly and intelligently."

Missouri has chosen only to appeal the Court of Appeals' invalidation of the public funding provision. . . . We accept, for purposes of decision, the State's claim that Section 188.205 "is not directed at the conduct of any physician or health care provider, private or public," but "is directed solely at those persons responsible for expending public funds."

. . . . A majority of the Court agrees . . . that the controversy over Section 188.205 is now moot. . . . We accordingly direct the Court of Appeals to vacate [annul] the judgment of the District Court with instructions to dismiss the relevant part of the complaint. . . .

Section 188.029 of the Missouri Act provides:

"Before a physician performs an abortion on a woman he has reason to believe is carrying an unborn child of twenty or more weeks gestational age, the physician shall first determine if the unborn child is viable by using and exercising that degree of care, skill, and proficiency commonly exercised by the ordinarily skillful, careful, and prudent physician engaged in similar practice under the same or similar conditions. In making this determination of viability, the physician shall perform or cause to be performed such medical examinations and tests as are necessary to make a finding of the gestational age, weight, and lung maturity of the unborn child and shall enter such findings and determination of viability in the medical record of the mother."

As with the preamble, the parties disagree over the meaning of this statutory provision. . . .

The Court of Appeals read Section 188.029 as requiring that after 20 weeks "doctors *must* perform tests to find gestational age, fetal weight and lung maturity." The court indicated that the tests needed to determine fetal weight at 20 weeks are "unreliable and inaccurate" and would add $125 to $250 to the cost of an abortion. It also stated that "amniocentesis, the only method available to determine lung maturity, is contrary to accepted medical practice until 28-30 weeks of gestation, expensive, and imposes significant health risks for both the pregnant woman and the fetus."

We must first determine the meaning of Section 188.029 under Missouri law. Our usual practice is to defer to the lower court's construction of a state statute, but we believe the Court of Appeals has "fallen into plain error" in this case. . . . The Court of Appeals' interpretation also runs "afoul of the well-established principle that statutes will be interpreted to avoid constitutional difficulties."

We think the viability-testing provision makes sense only if the second sentence is read to require only those tests that are useful to making subsidiary findings as to viability. If we construe [interpret] this provision to require a physician to perform those tests needed to make the three specified findings *in all circumstances*, including when the physician's reasonable professional judgment indicates that the tests would be irrelevant to determining viability or even dangerous to the mother and the fetus, the second sentence of Section 188.029 would conflict with the first sentence's *requirement* that a physician apply his reasonable professional skill and judgment. It would also be in-congruous to read this provision, especially the word "necessary," to require the performance of tests irrelevant to the expressed statutory purpose of determining viabili-ty. It thus seems clear to us that the Court of Appeals' construction of Section 188.029 violates well-accepted ca-nons of statutory interpretation used in the Missouri courts. . . .

The viability-testing provision of the Missouri Act is con-cerned with promoting the State's interest in potential hu-man life rather than in maternal health. Section 188.029 creates what is essentially a presumption of viability at 20 weeks, which the physician must rebut with tests indicat-ing that the fetus is not viable prior to performing an abortion. It also directs the physician's determination as to viability by specifying consideration, if feasible, of ges-tational age, fetal weight, and lung capacity. The District Court found that "the medical evidence is uncontradicted that a 20-week fetus is *not* viable," and that "23-1/2 to 24 weeks gestation is the earliest point in pregnancy where a reasonable possibility of viability exists." But it also found that there may be a 4-week error in estimating ges-tational age, which supports testing at 20 weeks.

In *Roe v. Wade,* the Court recognized that the State has "important and legitimate" interests in protecting mater-nal health and in the potentiality of human life. During the second trimester, the State "may, if it chooses, regulate the abortion procedure in ways that are reasonably related to maternal health." After viability, when the State's in-terest in potential human life was held to be compelling, the State "may, if it chooses, regulate, and even proscribe, abortion except where it is necessary, in appropriate medi-

cal judgment, for the preservation of the life or health of
the mother."

In *Colautti v. Franklin* . . . the Court held that a Pennsylvania statute regulating the standard of care to be used by
a physician performing an abortion of a possibly viable
fetus was void for vagueness. But in the course of reaching that conclusion, the Court reaffirmed its earlier statement in *Planned Parenthood of Central Missouri v. Danforth*, that "'the determination of whether a particular fetus is viable is, and must be, a matter for the judgment of
the responsible attending physician.'" . . . To the extent
that Section 188.029 regulates the method for determining viability, it undoubtedly does superimpose state regulation on the medical determination of whether a particular fetus is viable. The Court of Appeals and the District
Court thought it unconstitutional for this reason. To the
extent that the viability tests increase the cost of what are
in fact second-trimester abortions, their validity may also
be questioned under *Akron*, where the Court held that a
requirement that second trimester abortions must be performed in hospitals was invalid because it substantially increased the expense of those procedures.

. . . . *Stare decisis* [let past decisions stand] is a cornerstone of our legal system, but it has less power in constitutional cases, where, save for constitutional amendments,
this Court is the only body able to make needed changes.
We have not refrained from reconsideration of a prior
construction of the Constitution that has proved "unsound
in principle and unworkable in practice." We think the
Roe trimester framework falls into that category.

In the first place, the rigid *Roe* framework is hardly consistent with the notion of a Constitution cast in general terms, as ours is, and usually speaking in general principles, as ours does. The key elements of the *Roe* framework - trimesters and viability - are not found in the text of the Constitution or in any place else one would expect to find a constitutional principle. Since the bounds of the inquiry are essentially indeterminate, the result has been a web of legal rules that have become increasingly intricate, resembling a code of regulations rather than a body of constitutional doctrine. As Justice White has put it, the trimester framework has left this Court to serve as the country's "*ex officio* medical board with powers to approve or disapprove medical and operative practices and standards throughout the United States."

In the second place, we do not see why the State's interest in protecting potential human life should come into existence only at the point of viability, and that there should therefore be a rigid line allowing state regulation after viability but prohibiting it before viability. . . .

The tests that Section 188.029 requires the physician to perform are designed to determine viability. The State here has chosen viability as the point at which its interest in potential human life must be safeguarded. It is true that the tests in question increase the expense of abortion, and regulate the discretion of the physician in determining the viability of the fetus. Since the tests will undoubtedly show in many cases that the fetus is not viable, the tests will have been performed for what were in fact second-trimester abortions. But we are satisfied that the requirement of these tests permissibly furthers the State's

interest in protecting potential human life, and we there
fore believe Section 188.029 to be constitutional.

. . . . The Missouri testing requirement here is reasonably
designed to ensure that abortions are not performed
where the fetus is viable - an end which all concede is legitimate - and that is sufficient to sustain its constitutionality.

Justice Blackmun also accuses us [among other things] of
cowardice and illegitimacy in dealing with "the most politically divisive domestic legal issue of our time." . . . [T]he
goal of constitutional adjudication is surely not to remove
inexorably "politically divisive" issues from the ambit of
the legislative process, whereby the people through their
elected representatives deal with matters of concern to
them. The goal of constitutional adjudication is to hold
true the balance between that which the Constitution puts
beyond the reach of the democratic process and that
which it does not. We think we have done that today.
Justice Blackmun's suggestion that legislative bodies, in a
Nation where more than half of our population is women,
will treat our decision today as an invitation to enact abortion regulation reminiscent of the dark ages not only mis-
reads our views but does scant justice to those who serve
in such bodies and the people who elect them.

Both [Webster] and the United States as *Amicus Curiae*
[friends of the court] have urged that we overrule our decision in *Roe v. Wade.* The facts of the present case, however, differ from those at issue in *Roe.* Here, Missouri has
determined that viability is the point at which its interest
in potential human life must be safeguarded. In *Roe,* on
the other hand, the Texas statute criminalized the per-

formance of *all* abortions, except when the mother's life was at stake. This case therefore affords us no occasion to revisit the holding of *Roe*, which was that the Texas statute unconstitutionally infringed the right to an abortion derived from the Due Process Clause, and we leave it undisturbed. To the extent indicated in our opinion, we would modify and narrow *Roe* and succeeding cases.

Because none of the challenged provisions of the Missouri Act properly before us conflict with the Constitution, the judgment of the Court of Appeals is *reversed.*

JUSTICE O'CONNOR, concurring in part and concurring in the judgment: . . . . Nothing in the record before us or the opinions below indicates that subsections 1(1) and 1(2) of the preamble to Missouri's abortion regulation statute will affect a woman's decision to have an abortion. Justice Stevens . . . suggests that the preamble may also "interfer[e] with contraceptive choices," because certain contraceptive devices act on a female ovum after it has been fertilized by a male sperm. The Missouri Act defines "conception" as "the fertilization of the ovum of a female by a sperm of a male," and invests "unborn children" with "protectable interests in life, health, and well-being," from "the moment of conception. . . ." Justice Stevens asserts that any possible interference with a woman's right to use such post-fertilization contraceptive devices would be unconstitutional under *Griswold v. Connecticut*, and our subsequent contraception cases. . . . It may be correct that the use of postfertilization contraceptive devices is constitutionally protected by *Griswold* and its progeny but, as with a woman's abortion decision, nothing in the record or the opinions below indicates that the preamble will affect a woman's decision to practice con-

traception. . . . Neither is there any indication of the possibility that the preamble might be applied to prohibit the
performance of *in vitro* fertilization. I agree with the
Court, therefore, that all of these intimations of unconstitutionality are simply too hypothetical to support the use
of . . . remedies in this case.

Similarly, it seems to me to follow directly from our
previous decisions concerning state or federal funding of
abortions, *Harris v. McRae*, *Maher v. Roe*, and *Poelker v.
Doe*, that appellees' [Reproductive Health Services'] facial
challenge to the constitutionality of Missouri's ban on the
utilization of public facilities and the participation of
public employees in the performance of abortions not
necessary to save the life of the mother, cannot succeed.
Given Missouri's definition of "public facility" as "any
public institution, public facility, public equipment, or
any physical asset owned, leased, or controlled by this
state or any agency or political subdivisions thereof,"
there may be conceivable applications of the ban on the
use of public facilities that would be unconstitutional. . . .
Maher, *Poelker*, and *McRae* stand for the proposition that
some quite straightforward applications of the Missouri
ban on the use of public facilities for performing abortions would be constitutional and that is enough to defeat
[Reproductive Health Services'] assertion that the ban is
facially unconstitutional. . . . The fact that the [relevant
statute] might operate unconstitutionally under some conceivable set of circumstances is insufficient to render it
wholly invalid. . . .

I also agree with the Court that, under the interpretation
of Section 188.205 urged by the State and adopted by the
Court, there is no longer a case or controversy before us

over the constitutionality of that provision. I would note, however, that this interpretation of Section 188.205 is not binding on the Supreme Court of Missouri which has the final word on the meaning of that State's statutes. . . .

In its interpretation of Missouri's "determination of viability" provision, the plurality has proceeded in a manner unnecessary to deciding the question at hand. I agree with the plurality that it was plain error for the Court of Appeals to interpret the second sentence of Section 188.029 as meaning that "doctors *must* perform tests to find gestational age, fetal weight and lung maturity." When read together with the first sentence of Section 188.029 - which requires a physician to "determine if the unborn child is viable by using and exercising that degree of care, skill, and proficiency commonly exercised by the ordinary skillful, careful, and prudent physician engaged in similar practice under the same or similar conditions" - it would be contradictory nonsense to read the second sentence as requiring a physician to perform viability examinations and tests in situations where it would be careless and imprudent to do so. The plurality is quite correct: "the viability-testing provision makes sense only if the second sentence is read to require only those tests that are useful to making subsidiary findings as to viability," and, I would add, only those examinations and tests that it would not be imprudent or careless to perform in the particular medical situation before the physician.

Unlike the plurality, I do not understand these viability testing requirements to conflict with any of the Court's past decisions concerning state regulation of abortion. Therefore, there is no necessity to accept the State's invitation to reexamine the constitutional validity of *Roe v.*

Wade. Where there is no need to decide a constitutional question, it is a venerable principle of this Court's adjudicatory processes not to do so for "[t]he Court will not 'anticipate a question of constitutional law in advance of the necessity of deciding it.'" . . . The Court today has accepted the State's every interpretation of its abortion statute and has upheld, under our existing precedents, every provision of that statute which is properly before us. . . . When the constitutional invalidity of a State's abortion statute actually turns on the constitutional validity of *Roe v. Wade,* there will be time enough to reexamine *Roe.* And to do so carefully.

. . . . There is . . . no dispute between the parties before us over the constitutionality of the "presumption of viability at 20 weeks," created by the first sentence of Section 188.029. . . . As the plurality properly interprets the second sentence of Section 188.029, it does nothing more than delineate means by which the unchallenged 20-week presumption of viability may be overcome if those means are useful in doing so and can be prudently employed. . . .

I do not think the second sentence of Section 188.029, as interpreted by the Court, imposes a degree of state regulation on the medical determination of viability that in any way conflicts with prior decisions of this Court. . . . No decision of this Court has held that the State may not directly promote its interest in potential life when viability is possible. Quite the contrary. . . . Thus, all nine Members of the *Thornburgh* Court appear to have agreed that it is not constitutionally impermissible for the State to enact regulations designed to protect the State's interest in potential life when viability is possible. That is exactly what Missouri has done in Section 188.029.

.... All the second sentence of Section 188.029 does is to require, when not imprudent, the performance of "those tests that are useful to making *subsidiary* findings as to viability." Thus, consistent with *Colautti,* viability remains the "critical point" under Section 188.029.

Finally, and rather half-heartedly, the plurality suggests that the marginal increase in the cost of an abortion created by Missouri's viability testing provision may make Section 188.029, even as interpreted, suspect under this Court's decision in *Akron,* striking down a second-trimester hospitalization requirement. ...

It is clear to me that requiring the performance of examinations and tests useful to determining whether a fetus is viable, when viability is possible, and when it would not be medically imprudent to do so, does not impose an undue burden on a woman's abortion decision. On this ground alone I would reject the suggestion that Section 188.029 as interpreted is unconstitutional. ... The second-trimester hospitalization requirement struck down in *Akron* imposed, in the majority's view, "a heavy, and unnecessary, burden," more than doubling the cost of "women's access to a relatively inexpensive, otherwise accessible, and safe abortion procedure." By contrast, the cost of examinations and tests that could usefully and prudently be performed when a woman is 20-24 weeks pregnant to determine whether the fetus is viable would only marginally, if at all, increase the cost of an abortion. ...

Moreover, the examinations and tests required by Section 188.029 are to be performed when viability is possible. This feature of Section 188.029 distinguishes it from the second-trimester hospitalization requirement struck down by the *Akron* majority. . . . [B]ecause the Court of Appeals misinterpreted Section 188.029, and because, properly interpreted, Section 188.029 is not inconsistent with any of this Court's prior precedents, I would reverse the decision of the Court of Appeals. . . .

JUSTICE SCALIA, concurring in part and concurring in the judgment: . . . . I share Justice Blackmun's view that it effectively would overrule *Roe v. Wade*. I think that should be done, but would do it more explicitly. Since today we contrive to avoid doing it, and indeed to avoid almost any decision of national import, I need not set forth my reasons. . . .

The outcome of today's case will doubtless be heralded as a triumph of judicial statesmanship. It is not that, unless it is statesmanlike needlessly to prolong this Court's self-awarded sovereignty over a field where it has little proper business since the answers to most of the cruel questions posed are political and not juridical - a sovereignty which therefore quite properly, but to the great damage of the Court, makes it the object of the sort of organized public pressure that political institutions in a democracy ought to receive.

. . . . By finessing *Roe* we do not . . . adhere to the strict and venerable rule that we should avoid "'decid[ing] questions of a constitutional nature.'" We have not disposed of this case on some statutory or procedural ground, but have decided, and could not avoid deciding, whether the Missouri statute meets the requirements of the United States Constitution. The only choice available is whether, in deciding that constitutional question, we should use *Roe v. Wade* as the benchmark, or something else. What is involved, therefore, is not the rule of avoiding constitutional issues where possible, but the quite separate principle that we will not "'formulate a rule of constitutional law broader than is required by the precise facts to which it is to be applied.'" The latter is a sound general principle, but one often departed from when good reason exists. . . .

The Court has often spoken more broadly than needed in precisely the fashion at issue here, announcing a new rule of constitutional law when it could have reached the identical result by applying the rule thereby displaced. . . . It is rare, of course, that the Court goes out of its way to *acknowledge* that its judgment could have been reached under the old constitutional rule, making its adoption of the new one unnecessary to the decision, but even such explicit acknowledgment is not unheard of. . . . It would be wrong, in any decision, to ignore the reality that our policy not to "formulate a rule of constitutional law broader than is required by the precise facts" has a frequently applied good-cause exception. But it seems particularly perverse to convert the policy into an absolute in the present case, in order to place beyond reach the inexpressibly "broader-than-was-required-by-the-precise-facts" structure established by *Roe v. Wade.*

The real question, then, is whether there are valid reasons to go beyond the most stingy possible holding today. It seems to me there are not only valid but compelling ones. Ordinarily, speaking no more broadly than is absolutely required avoids throwing settled law into confusion; doing so today preserves a chaos that is evident to anyone who can read and count. Alone sufficient to justify a broad holding is the fact that our retaining control, through *Roe,* of what I believe to be, and many of our citizens recognize to be, a political issue, continuously distorts the public perception of the role of this Court. We can now look forward to at least another Term with carts full of mail from the public, and streets full of demonstrators, urging us - their unelected and life-tenured judges who have been awarded those extraordinary, undemocratic characteristics precisely in order that we might follow the law despite the popular will - to follow the popular will. Indeed, I expect we can look forward to even more of that than before, given our indecisive decision today. And if these reasons for taking the unexceptional course of reaching a broader holding are not enough, then consider the nature of the constitutional question we avoid: In most cases, we do no harm by not speaking more broadly than the decision requires. Anyone affected by the conduct that the avoided holding would have prohibited will be able to challenge it himself, and have his day in court to make the argument. Not so with respect to the harm that many States believed, pre-*Roe*, and many may continue to believe, is caused by largely unrestricted abortion. That will continue to occur if the States have the constitutional power to prohibit it, and would do so, but we skillfully avoid telling them so. Perhaps those abortions cannot constitutionally be proscribed. That is surely an arguable question, the question that reconsideration of *Roe v. Wade* entails. But what is not at all arguable, it seems to me, is that we should decide now and not insist that we be run into a corner before we grudgingly yield up our judgment. The only sound reason for the latter course is to prevent a change in the law - but to think that desirable begs the question to be decided.

It was an arguable question today whether Section
188.029 of the Missouri law contravened [went against]
this Court's understanding of *Roe v. Wade*, and I would
have examined *Roe* rather than examining the contraven-
tion. Given the Court's newly contracted abstemiousness,
what will it take, one must wonder, to permit us to reach
that fundamental question? The result of our vote today
is that we will not reconsider that prior opinion, even if
most of the Justices think it is wrong, unless we have before us a statute that in fact contradicts it - and even then
(under our newly discovered "no-broader-than-necessary"
requirement) only minor problematical aspects of *Roe*
will be reconsidered, unless one expects State legislatures
to adopt provisions whose compliance with *Roe* cannot
even be argued with a straight face. It thus appears that
the mansion of constitutionalized abortion-law, construct-
ed overnight in *Roe v. Wade*, must be disassembled doorjamb by doorjamb, and never entirely brought down, no
matter how wrong it may be.

Of the four courses we might have chosen today - to reaffirm *Roe*, to overrule it explicitly, to overrule it *sub silen-
tio* [without explanation], or to avoid the question - the
last is the least responsible. On the question of the constitutionality of Section 188.029, I concur in the judgment
of the Court and strongly dissent from the manner in
which it has been reached.

JUSTICE BLACKMUN (joined by Justices Brennan and
Marshall), concurring in part and dissenting in part: Today, *Roe v. Wade* and the fundamental constitutional right
of women to decide whether to terminate a pregnancy,
survive but are not secure. Although the Court extricates
itself from this case without making a single, even incre-

mental, change in the law of abortion, the plurality and
Justice Scalia would overrule *Roe* (the first silently, the
other explicitly) and would return to the States virtually
unfettered authority to control the quintessentially intimate, personal, and life-directing decision whether to carry a fetus to term. Although today, no less than yester-
day, the Constitution and the decisions of this Court prohibit a State from enacting laws that inhibit women from
the meaningful exercise of that right, a plurality of this
Court implicitly invites every state legislature to enact
more and more restrictive abortion regulations in order to
provoke more and more test cases, in the hope that some-
time down the line the Court will return the law of procreative freedom to the severe limitations that generally
prevailed in this country before January 22, 1973. Never
in my memory has a plurality announced a judgment of
this Court that so foments disregard for the law and for
our standing decisions.

Nor in my memory has a plurality gone about its business
in such a deceptive fashion. At every level of its review,
from its effort to read the real meaning out of the Missouri statute, to its intended evisceration of precedents
and its deafening silence about the constitutional protections that it would jettison, the plurality obscures the portent of its analysis. With feigned restraint, the plurality
announces that its analysis leaves *Roe* "undisturbed," al-
beit "modif[ied] and narrow[ed]." But this disclaimer is
totally meaningless. The plurality opinion is filled with
winks, and nods, and knowing glances to those who would
do away with *Roe* explicitly, but turns a stone face to anyone in search of what the plurality conceives as the scope
of a woman's right under the Due Process Clause to terminate a pregnancy free from the coercive and brooding

influence of the State. The simple truth is that *Roe* would not survive the plurality's analysis, and that the plurality provides no substitute for *Roe*'s protective umbrella.

I fear for the future. I fear for the liberty and equality of the millions of women who have lived and come of age in the 16 years since *Roe* was decided. I fear for the integrity of, and public esteem for, this Court.

I dissent.

The Chief Justice parades through the four challenged sections of the Missouri statute *seriatim* [one by one]. I shall not do this.... Although I disagree with the Court's consideration of Sections 188.205, 188.210, and 188.215, and am especially disturbed by its misapplication of our past decisions in upholding Missouri's ban on the performance of abortions at "public facilities," its discussion of these provisions is merely prologue to the plurality's consideration of the statute's viability-testing requirement, Section 188.029 - the only section of the Missouri statute that the plurality construes [interprets] as implicating *Roe* itself. There, tucked away at the end of its opinion, the plurality suggests a radical reversal of the law of abortion; and there, primarily, I direct my attention.

In the plurality's view, the viability-testing provision imposes a burden on second-trimester abortions as a way of furthering the State's interest in protecting the potential life of the fetus. Since under the *Roe* framework, the State may not fully regulate abortion in the interest of potential life (as opposed to maternal health) until the third trimester, the plurality finds it necessary, in order to save the Missouri testing provision, to throw out *Roe's* trimester framework. In flat contradiction to *Roe*, the plurality concludes that the State's interest in potential life is compelling before viability, and upholds the testing provision because it "permissibly furthers" that state interest.

At the outset, I note that in its haste to limit abortion rights, the plurality compounds the errors of its analysis by needlessly reaching out to address constitutional questions that are not actually presented. The conflict between Section 188.029 and *Roe's* trimester framework, which purportedly drives the plurality to reconsider our past decisions, is a contrived conflict: the product of an aggressive misreading of the viability-testing requirement and a needlessly wooden application of the *Roe* framework.

The plurality's reading of Section 188.029 is irreconcilable with the plain language of the statute and is in derogation of this Court's settled view that "'district courts and courts of appeals are better schooled in and more able to interpret the laws of their respective States.'" Abruptly setting aside the construction of Section 188.029 adopted by both the District Court and Court of Appeals as "plain error," the plurality reads the viability-testing provision as requiring only that before a physician may perform an abortion on a woman whom he believes to be carrying a fetus of 20 or more weeks gestational age, the doctor must determine whether the fetus is viable and, as part of that exercise, must, to the extent feasible and consistent with sound medical practice, conduct tests necessary to make findings of gestational age, weight, and lung maturity. But the plurality's reading of the provision, according to which the statute requires the physician to perform tests only in order to determine *viability*, ignores the statutory language explicitly directing that "the physician *shall* perform or cause to be performed such medical examinations and tests as are *necessary to make a finding of the gestational age, weight, and lung maturity* of the unborn child and *shall* enter such findings" in the mother's medical record. The statute's plain language requires the physician to undertake whatever tests are necessary to determine gestational age, weight, and lung maturity, regardless of whether these tests are necessary to a finding of viability, and regardless of whether the tests subject the pregnant woman or the fetus to additional health risks or add substantially to the cost of an abortion.

Had the plurality read the statute as written, it would have had no cause to reconsider the *Roe* framework. As properly construed, the viability-testing provision does not pass constitutional muster under even a rational-basis standard, the least restrictive level of review applied by this Court. By mandating tests to determine fetal weight and lung maturity for every fetus thought to be more than 20 weeks gestational age, the statute requires physicians to undertake procedures, such as amniocentesis, that, in the situation presented, have no medical justification, impose significant additional health risks on both the pregnant woman and the fetus, and bear no rational relation to the State's interest in protecting fetal life. As written, Section 188.029 is an arbitrary imposition of discomfort, risk, and expense, furthering no discernible interest except to make the procurement of an abortion as arduous and difficult as possible. Thus, were it not for the plurality's tortured effort to avoid the plain import of Section 188.029, it could have struck down the testing provision as patently irrational irrespective of the *Roe* framework.

. . . . No one contests that under the *Roe* framework the State, in order to promote its interest in potential human life, may regulate and even proscribe nontherapeutic abortions once the fetus becomes viable. If, as the plurality appears to hold, the testing provision simply requires a physician to use appropriate and medically sound tests to determine whether the fetus is actually viable when the estimated gestational age is greater than 20 weeks . . . , then I see little or no conflict with *Roe*. Nothing in *Roe*, or any of its progeny, holds that a State may not effectuate its compelling interest in the potential life of a viable fetus by seeking to ensure that no viable fetus is mistakenly aborted because of the inherent lack of precision in estimates of gestational age. A requirement that a physician make a finding of viability, one way or the other, for every fetus that falls within the range of possible viability does no more than preserve the State's recognized authority. Although, as the plurality correctly points out, such a testing requirement would have the effect of imposing additional costs on second-trimester abortions where the tests indicated that the fetus was not viable; these costs would be merely incidental to, and a necessary accommodation of, the State's unquestioned right to prohibit nontherapeutic abortions after the point of viability. In short, the testing provision, as [interpreted] by the plurality is consistent with the *Roe* framework and could be upheld effortlessly under current doctrine.

. . . . By distorting the statute, the plurality manages to avoid invalidating the testing provision on what should have been noncontroversial constitutional grounds; having done so, however, the plurality rushes headlong into a much deeper constitutional thicket, brushing past an obvious basis for upholding Section 188.029 in search of a pretext for scuttling the trimester framework. . . .

Having set up the conflict between Section 188.029 and the *Roe* trimester framework, the plurality summarily discards *Roe*'s analytic core as "'unsound in principle and unworkable in practice.'" This is so, the plurality claims, because the key elements of the framework do not appear in the text of the Constitution, because the framework more closely resembles a regulatory code than a body of constitutional doctrine, and because under the framework the State's interest in potential human life is considered compelling only after viability, when, in fact, that interest is equally compelling throughout pregnancy. The plurality does not bother to explain these alleged flaws in *Roe*. Bald assertion masquerades as reasoning. The object, quite clearly, is not to persuade, but to prevail.

The plurality opinion is far more remarkable for the arguments that it does not advance than for those that it does. The plurality does not even mention, much less join, the true jurisprudential debate underlying this case: whether the Constitution includes an "unenumerated" general right to privacy as recognized in many of our decisions, most notably *Griswold v. Connecticut* and *Roe*, and, more specifically, whether, and to what extent, such a right to privacy extends to matters of childbearing and family life, including abortion. These are questions of unsurpassed significance in this Court's interpretation of the Constitution, and mark the battleground upon which this case was fought. . . .

But rather than arguing that the text of the Constitution makes no mention of the right to privacy, the plurality complains that the critical elements of the *Roe* framework - trimesters and viability - do not appear in the Constitution and are, therefore, somehow inconsistent with a Constitution cast in general terms. Were this a true concern, we would have to abandon most of our constitutional jurisprudence. As the plurality well knows, or should know, the "critical elements" of countless constitutional doctrines nowhere appear in the Constitution's text. The Constitution makes no mention, for example, of the First Amendment's "actual malice" standard for proving certain libels, or of the standard for determining when speech is obscene. Similarly, the Constitution makes no mention of the rational-basis test, or the specific verbal formulations of intermediate and strict scrutiny by which this Court evaluates claims under the Equal Protection Clause. The reason is simple. Like the *Roe* framework, these tests or standards are not, and do not purport to be, rights protected by the Constitution. Rather, they are judge-made methods for evaluating and measuring the strength and scope of constitutional rights or for balancing the constitutional rights of individuals against the competing interests of government.

With respect to the *Roe* framework, the general constitutional principle, indeed the fundamental constitutional right, for which it was developed is the right to privacy, a species of "liberty" protected by the Due Process Clause, which under our past decisions safeguards the right of women to exercise some control over their own role in procreation. As we recently reaffirmed in *Thornburgh v. American College of Obstetricians and Gynecologists*, few decisions are "more basic to individual dignity and autonomy" or more appropriate to that "certain private sphere of individual liberty" that the Constitution reserves from the intrusive reach of government than the right to make the uniquely personal, intimate, and self-defining decision whether to end a pregnancy. It is this general principle, the "'moral fact that a person belongs to himself and not others nor to society as a whole,'" that is found in the Constitution. The trimester framework simply defines and limits that right to privacy in the abortion context to accommodate, not destroy, a State's legitimate interest in protecting the health of pregnant women and in preserving potential human life. Fashioning such accommodations between individual rights and the legitimate interests of government, establishing benchmarks and standards with which to evaluate the competing claims of individuals and government, lies at the very heart of constitutional adjudication.   To the extent that the trimester framework is useful in this enterprise, it is not only consistent with constitutional interpretation, but necessary to the wise and just exercise of this Court's paramount authority to define the scope of constitutional rights.

The plurality next alleges that the result of the trimester framework has "been a web of legal rules that have become increasingly intricate, resembling a code of regulations rather than a body of constitutional doctrine." . . .

That numerous constitutional doctrines result in narrow differentiations between similar circumstances does not mean that this Court has abandoned adjudication in favor of regulation. Rather, these careful distinctions reflect the process of constitutional adjudication itself, which is often highly fact-specific, requiring such determinations as whether state laws are "unduly burdensome" or "reasonable" or bear a "rational" or "necessary" relation to asserted state interests. In a recent due process case, The Chief Justice wrote for the Court: "[M]any branches of the law abound in nice distinctions that may be troublesome but have been thought nonetheless necessary: 'I do not think we need trouble ourselves with the thought that my view depends upon differences of degree. The whole law does so as soon as it is civilized.'"

.... If, in delicate and complicated areas of constitutional law, our legal judgments "have become increasingly intricate," it is not, as the plurality contends, because we have overstepped our judicial role. Quite the opposite: the rules are intricate because we have remained conscientious in our duty to do justice carefully, especially when fundamental rights rise or fall with our decisions.

Finally, the plurality asserts that the trimester framework cannot stand because the State's interest in potential life is compelling throughout pregnancy, not merely after viability. The opinion contains not one word of rationale for its view of the State's interest. This "it is so because we say so" jurisprudence constitutes nothing other than an attempted exercise of brute force; reason, much less persuasion, has no place.

.... I remain convinced ... that the *Roe* framework, and the viability standard in particular, fairly, sensibly, and effectively functions to safeguard the constitutional liberties of pregnant women while recognizing and accommodating the State's interest in potential human life. The viability line reflects the biological facts and truths of fetal development; it marks that threshold moment prior to which a fetus cannot survive separate from the woman and cannot reasonably and objectively be regarded as a subject of rights or interests distinct from, or paramount to, those of the pregnant woman. At the same time, the viability standard takes account of the undeniable fact that as the fetus evolves into its postnatal form, and as it loses its dependence on the uterine environment, the State's interest in the fetus' potential human life, and in fostering a regard for human life in general, becomes compelling. As a practical matter, because viability follows "quickening" - the point at which a woman feels movement in her womb - and because viability occurs no earlier than 23 weeks gestational age, it establishes an easily applicable standard for regulating abortion while providing a pregnant woman ample time to exercise her fundamental right with her responsible physician to terminate her pregnancy. Although I have stated previously for a majority of this Court that "[c]onstitutional rights do not always have easily ascertainable boundaries," to seek and establish those boundaries remains the special responsibility of this Court. In *Roe*, we discharged that responsibility as logic and science compelled. The plurality today advances not one reasonable argument as to why our judgment in that case was wrong and should be abandoned.

Having contrived an opportunity to reconsider the *Roe* framework, and then having discarded that framework, the plurality finds the testing provision unobjectionable because it "permissibly furthers the State's interest in protecting potential human life." This newly minted standard is circular and totally meaningless. Whether a challenged abortion regulation "permissibly furthers" a legitimate state interest is the *question* that courts must answer in abortion cases, not the standard for courts to apply. . . .

The "permissibly furthers" standard has no independent meaning, and consists of nothing other than what a majority of this Court may believe at any given moment in any given case. The plurality's novel test appears to be nothing more than a dressed-up version of rational-basis review, this Court's most lenient level of scrutiny. One thing is clear, however: were the plurality's "permissibly furthers" standard adopted by the Court, for all practical purposes, *Roe* would be overruled.

The "permissibly furthers" standard completely disregards the irreducible minimum of *Roe*: the Court's recognition that a woman has a limited fundamental constitutional right to decide whether to terminate a pregnancy. . . . Since, in the plurality's view, the State's interest in potential life is compelling as of the moment of conception, and is therefore served only if abortion is abolished, every hindrance to a woman's ability to obtain an abortion must be "permissible." Indeed, the more severe the hindrance, the more effectively (and permissibly) the State's interest would be furthered. A tax on abortions or a criminal prohibition would both satisfy the plurality's standard. So, for that matter, would a requirement that a pregnant woman memorize and recite today's plurality opinion before seeking an abortion.

The plurality pretends that *Roe* survives, explaining that the facts of this case differ from those in *Roe*. . . . The plurality repudiates every principle for which *Roe* stands. . . . It is impossible to read the plurality opinion and especially its final paragraph, without recognizing its implicit invitation to every State to enact more and more restrictive abortion laws, and to assert their interest in potential life as of the moment of conception. All these

laws will satisfy the plurality's non-scrutiny, until some-
time, a new regime of old dissenters and new appointees
will declare what the plurality intends: that *Roe* is no
longer good law.

Thus, "not with a bang, but a whimper," the plurality discards a landmark case of the last generation, and casts into
darkness the hopes and visions of every woman in this
country who had come to believe that the Constitution
guaranteed her the right to exercise some control over her
unique ability to bear children. The plurality does so either oblivious or insensitive to the fact that millions of
women, and their families, have ordered their lives around
the right to reproductive choice, and that this right has become vital to the full participation of women in the economic and political walks of American life. The plurality
would clear the way once again for government to force
upon women the physical labor and specific and direct
medical and psychological harms that may accompany carrying a fetus to term. The plurality would clear the way
again for the State to conscript a woman's body and to
force upon her a "distressful life and future."

The result, as we know from experience, would be that every year hundreds of thousands of women, in desperation,
would defy the law, and place their health and safety in
the unclean and unsympathetic hands of back-alley abor-
tionists, or they would attempt to perform abortions upon
themselves, with disastrous results. Every year, many
women, especially poor and minority women, would die or
suffer debilitating physical trauma, all in the name of en-
forced morality or religious dictates or lack of compassion, as it may be.

Of the aspirations and settled understandings of American women, of the inevitable and brutal consequences of what it is doing, the tough-approach plurality utters not a word. This silence is callous. It is also profoundly destructive of this Court as an institution. To overturn a constitutional decision is a rare and grave undertaking. To overturn a constitutional decision that secured a fundamental personal liberty to millions of persons would be unprecedented in our 200 years of constitutional history. Although the doctrine of *stare decisis* applies with somewhat diminished force in constitutional cases generally, even in ordinary constitutional cases "any departure from . . . *stare decisis* demands special justification." This requirement of justification applies with unique force where, as here, the Court's abrogation of precedent would destroy people's firm belief, based on past decisions of this Court, that they possess an unabridgeable right to undertake certain conduct.

. . . . [T]he plurality pretends that it leaves *Roe* standing, and refuses even to discuss the real issue underlying this case: whether the Constitution includes an unenumerated right to privacy that encompasses a woman's right to decide whether to terminate a pregnancy. . . .

This comes at a cost. . . . Today's decision involves the most politically divisive domestic legal issue of our time. By refusing to explain or to justify its proposed revolutionary revision in the law of abortion, and by refusing to abide not only by our precedents [past decisions], but also by our canons for reconsidering those precedents, the plurality invites charges of cowardice and illegitimacy to our door. I cannot say that these would be undeserved.

For today, at least, the law of abortion stands undisturbed. For today, the women of this Nation still retain the liberty to control their destinies. But the signs are evident and very ominous, and a chill wind blows.

JUSTICE STEVENS, concurring in part and dissenting in part: . . . . In this case, I agree with the Court of Appeals and the District Court that the meaning of the second sentence of Section 188.029 is too plain to be ignored. The sentence twice uses the mandatory term "shall," and contains no qualifying language. If it is implicitly limited to tests that are useful in determining viability, it adds nothing to the requirement imposed by the preceding sentence.

My interpretation of the plain language is supported by the structure of the statute as a whole, particularly the preamble, which "finds" that life "begins at conception" and further commands that state laws shall be construed to provide the maximum protection to "the unborn child at every stage of development." I agree with the District Court that "[o]bviously, the purpose of this law is to protect the potential life of the fetus, rather than to safeguard maternal health." A literal reading of the statute tends to accomplish that goal. Thus it is not "incongruous" to assume that the Missouri Legislature was trying to protect the potential human life of nonviable fetuses by making the abortion decision more costly. On the contrary, I am satisfied that the Court of Appeals, as well as the District Court, correctly concluded that the Missouri Legislature meant exactly what it said in the second sentence of Section 188.029. I am also satisfied . . . that the testing provision is manifestly unconstitutional. . . .

The Missouri statute defines "conception" as "the fertilization of the ovum of a female by a sperm of a male," even
though standard medical texts equate "conception" with
implantation in the uterus, occurring about six days after
fertilization. Missouri's declaration therefore implies regulation not only of previability abortions, but also of common forms of contraception such as the IUD and the
morning-after pill. . . .

To the extent that the Missouri statute interferes with
contraceptive choices, I have no doubt that it is unconstitutional under the Court's holdings in *Griswold v. Connecticut, Eisenstadt v. Baird,* and *Carey v. Population
Services International.* . . .

One might argue that the *Griswold* holding applies to devices "preventing conception," - that is, fertilization - but
not to those preventing implantation, and therefore, that
Griswold does not protect a woman's choice to use an IUD
or take a morning-after pill. There is unquestionably a
theological basis for such an argument, just as there was
unquestionably a theological basis for the Connecticut
statute that the Court invalidated in *Griswold.* Our jurisprudence, however, has consistently required a secular basis for valid legislation. Because I am not aware of any
secular basis for differentiating between contraceptive
procedures that are effective immediately before and
those that are effective immediately after fertilization, I
believe it inescapably follows that the preamble to the
Missouri statute is invalid under *Griswold* and its progeny.

Indeed, I am persuaded that the absence of any secular
purpose for the legislative declarations that life begins at

conception and that conception occurs at fertilization makes the relevant portion of the preamble invalid under the Establishment Clause of the First Amendment to the Federal Constitution. This conclusion does not, and could not, rest on the fact that the statement happens to coincide with the tenets of certain religions, or on the fact that the legislators who voted to enact it may have been motivated by religious considerations. Rather, it rests on the fact that the preamble, an unequivocal endorsement of a religious tenet of some but by no means all Christian faiths, serves no identifiable secular purpose. That fact alone compels a conclusion that the statute violates the Establishment Clause.

. . . . The preamble to the Missouri statute endorses the theological position that there is the same secular interest in preserving the life of a fetus during the first 40 or 80 days of pregnancy as there is after viability - indeed, after the time when the fetus has become a "person" with legal rights protected by the Constitution. To sustain that position as a matter of law, I believe Missouri has the burden of identifying the secular interests that differentiate the first 40 days of pregnancy from the period immediately before or after fertilization when, as *Griswold* and related cases establish, the Constitution allows the use of contraceptive procedures to prevent potential life from developing into full personhood. Focusing our attention on the first several weeks of pregnancy is especially appropriate because that is the period when the vast majority of abortions are actually performed.

As a secular matter, there is an obvious difference between the state interest in protecting the freshly fertilized egg and the state interest in protecting a 9-month-gestated, fully sentient fetus on the eve of birth. There can be no interest in protecting the newly fertilized egg from physical pain or mental anguish, because the capacity for such suffering does not yet exist; respecting a developed fetus, however, that interest is valid. In fact, if one rescinds the theological concept of ensoulment - or one accepts St. Thomas Aquinas' view that ensoulment does not occur for at least 40 days - a State has no greater secular interest in protecting the potential life of an embryo that is still "seed" than in protecting the potential life of a sperm or an unfertilized ovum.

There have been times in history when military and economic interests would have been served by an increase in population. No one argues today, however, that Missouri can assert a societal interest in increasing its population as its secular reason for fostering potential life. Indeed, our national policy, as reflected in legislation the Court upheld last Term, is to prevent the potential life that is produced by "pregnancy and childbirth among unmarried adolescents." If the secular analysis were based on a strict balancing of fiscal costs and benefits, the economic costs of unlimited childbearing would outweigh those of abortion. There is, of course, an important and unquestionably valid secular interest in "protecting a young pregnant woman from the consequences of an incorrect decision." Although that interest is served by a requirement that the woman receive medical and, in appropriate circumstances, parental, advice, it does not justify the state legislature's official endorsement of the theological tenet embodied in Sections 1.205.1(1), (2).

.... Bolstering my conclusion that the preamble violates the First Amendment is the fact that the intensely divisive character of much of the national debate over the abortion issue reflects the deeply held religious convictions of many participants in the debate. The Missouri Legislature may not inject its endorsement of a particular religious tradition into this debate, for "[t]he Establishment Clause does not allow public bodies to foment such disagreement."

In my opinion the preamble to the Missouri statute is unconstitutional for two reasons. To the extent that it has substantive impact on the freedom to use contraceptive procedures, it is inconsistent with the central holding in *Griswold.* To the extent that it merely makes "legislative findings without operative effect," as the State argues, it violates the Establishment Clause of the First Amendment. Contrary to the theological "finding" of the Missouri Legislature, a woman's constitutionally protected liberty encompasses the right to act on her own belief that - to paraphrase St. Thomas Aquinas - until a seed has acquired the powers of sensation and movement, the life of a human being has not yet begun.

THE U.S. CONSTITUTION

THE U.S. CONSTITUTION

PREAMBLE

We the people of the United States, in order to form a more perfect union, establish justice, insure domestic tranquility, provide for the common defense, promote the general welfare, and secure the blessings of liberty to ourselves and our posterity, do ordain and establish this Constitution for the United States of America.

ARTICLE I

Section 1. All legislative powers herein granted shall be vested in a Congress of the United States, which shall consist of a Senate and House of Representatives.

Section 2. (1) The House of Representatives shall be composed of members chosen every second year by the people of the several states, and the electors in each state shall have the qualifications requisite for electors of the most numerous branch of the State Legislature.

(2) No person shall be a Representative who shall not have attained to the age of twenty-five years, and been seven years a citizen of the United States, and who shall not, when elected, be an inhabitant of that state in which he shall be chosen.

(3) Representatives and direct taxes shall be apportioned among the several states which may be included within this union, according to their respective numbers, which shall be determined by adding to the whole number of free persons, including those bound to service for a term of years, and excluding Indians not taxed, three-fifths of all other persons. The actual enumeration shall be made

within three years after the first meeting of the Congress of the United States, and within every subsequent term of ten years, in such manner as they shall by law direct. The number of Representatives shall not exceed one for every thirty thousand, but each state shall have at least one Representative; and until such enumeration shall be made, the State of New Hampshire shall be entitled to choose three, Massachusetts eight, Rhode Island and Providence Plantations one, Connecticut five, New York six, New Jersey four, Pennsylvania eight, Delaware one, Maryland six, Virginia ten, North Carolina five, South Carolina five, and Georgia three.

(4) When vacancies happen in the representation from any state, the executive authority thereof shall issue writs of election to fill such vacancies.

(5) The House of Representatives shall choose their Speaker and other Officers; and shall have the sole power of impeachment.

Section 3. (1) The Senate of the United States shall be composed of two Senators from each state, chosen by the legislature thereof, for six years; and each Senator shall have one vote.

(2) Immediately after they shall be assembled in consequence of the first election, they shall be divided as equally as may be into three classes. The seats of the Senators of the first class shall be vacated at the expiration of the second year, of the second class at the expiration of the fourth year, and of the third class at the expiration of the sixth year, so that one-third may be chosen every second year; and if vacancies happen by resignation, or otherwise, during the recess of the legislature of any state, the execu-

tive thereof may make temporary appointments until the next meeting of the legislature, which shall then fill such vacancies.

(3) No person shall be a Senator who shall not have attained to the age of thirty years, and been nine years a citizen of the United States, and who shall not, when elected, be an inhabitant of that state for which he shall be chosen.

(4) The Vice President of the United States shall be President of the Senate, but shall have no vote, unless they be equally divided.

(5) The Senate shall choose their other Officers, and also a President pro tempore, in the absence of the Vice President, or when he shall exercise the Office of President of the United States.

(6) The Senate shall have the sole power to try all impeachments. When sitting for that purpose, they shall be on oath or affirmation. When the President of the United States is tried, the Chief Justice shall preside: and no person shall be convicted without the concurrence of two-thirds of the members present.

(7) Judgment in cases of impeachment shall not extend further than to removal from office, and disqualification to hold and enjoy any office of honor, trust, or profit under the United States: but the party convicted shall nevertheless be liable and subject to indictment, trial, judgment, and punishment, according to law.

Section 4. (1) The times, places and manner of holding
elections for Senators and Representatives, shall be prescribed in each state by the legislature thereof; but the
Congress may at any time by law make or alter such regulations, except as to the places of choosing Senators.

(2) The Congress shall assemble at least once in every
year, and such meeting shall be on the first Monday in
December, unless they shall by law appoint a different
day.

Section 5. (1) Each House shall be the judge of the elections, returns, and qualifications of its own members, and
a majority of each shall constitute a quorum to do business; but a smaller number may adjourn from day to day,
and may be authorized to compel the attendance of absent
members, in such manner, and under such penalties as
each House may provide.

(2) Each House may determine the rules of its proceedings, punish its members for disorderly behavior, and,
with the concurrence of two-thirds, expel a member.

(3) Each House shall keep a journal of its proceedings,
and from time to time publish the same, excepting such
parts as may in their judgment require secrecy; and the
yeas and nays of the members of either House on any
question shall, at the desire of one-fifth of those present,
be entered on the journal.

(4) Neither House, during the Session of Congress, shall,
without the consent of the other, adjourn for more than
three days, nor to any other place than that in which the
two Houses shall be sitting.

Section 6. (1) The Senators and Representatives shall receive a compensation for their services, to be ascertained by law, and paid out of the Treasury of the United States. They shall in all cases, except treason, felony and breach of the peace, be privileged from arrest during their attendance at the session of their respective Houses, and in going to and returning from the same; and for any speech or debate in either House, they shall not be questioned in any other place.

(2) No Senator or Representative shall, during the time for which he was elected, be appointed to any civil office under the authority of the United States, which shall have been created, or the emoluments whereof shall have been increased during such time and no person holding any office under the United States, shall be a member of either House during his continuance in office.

Section 7. (1) All bills for raising revenue shall originate in the House of Representatives; but the Senate may propose or concur with amendments as on other bills.

(2) Every bill which shall have passed the House of Representatives and the Senate, shall, before it become a law, be presented to the President of the United States; if he approve he shall sign it, but if not he shall return it, with his objections to the House in which it shall have originated, who shall enter the objections at large on their journal, and proceed to reconsider it. If after such reconsideration two-thirds of that House shall agree to pass the bill, it shall be sent together with the objections, to the other House, by which it shall likewise be reconsidered, and if approved by two-thirds of that House, it shall become a law. But in all such cases the votes of both Houses shall be determined by yeas and nays, and the names of the per-

sons voting for and against the bill shall be entered on the journal of each House respectively. If any bill shall not be returned by the President within ten days (Sundays excepted) after it shall have been presented to him, the same shall be a law, in like manner as if he had signed it, unless the Congress by their adjournment prevent its return in which case it shall not be a law.

(3) Every order, resolution, or vote, to which the concurrence of the Senate and House of Representatives may be necessary (except on a question of adjournment) shall be presented to the President of the United States; and before the same shall take effect, shall be approved by him, or being disapproved by him, shall be repassed by two-thirds of the Senate and House of Representatives, according to the rules and limitations prescribed in the case of a bill.

Section 8. (1) The Congress shall have the power to lay and collect taxes, duties, imposts and excises, to pay the debts and provide for the common defense and general welfare of the United States; but all duties, imposts and excises shall be uniform throughout the United States;

(2) To borrow money on the credit of the United States;

(3) To regulate commerce with foreign nations, and among the several states, and with the Indian Tribes;

(4) To establish an uniform Rule of Naturalization, and uniform laws on the subject of bankruptcies throughout the United States;

(5) To coin money, regulate the value thereof, and of foreign coin, and fix the standard of weights and measures;

(6) To provide for the punishment of counterfeiting the securities and current coin of the United States;

(7) To establish Post Offices and Post Roads;

(8) To promote the progress of science and useful arts, by securing for limited times to authors and inventors the exclusive right to their respective writings and discoveries;

(9) To constitute tribunals inferior to the Supreme Court;

(10) To define and punish piracies and felonies committed on the high seas, and offenses against the Law of Nations;

(11) To declare war, grant Letters of marque and reprisal, and make rules concerning captures on land and water;

(12) To raise and support armies, but no appropriation of money to that use shall be for a longer term than two years;

(13) To provide and maintain a Navy;

(14) To make rules for the government and regulation of the land and naval forces;

(15) To provide for calling forth the Militia to execute the laws of the Union, suppress insurrections and repel invasions;

(16) To provide for organizing, arming, and disciplining, the Militia, and for governing such part of them as may be employed in the service of the United States, reserving to the states respectively, the appointment of the Officers,

and the authority of training the Militia according to the discipline prescribed by Congress;

(17) To exercise exclusive legislation in all cases whatsoever, over such district (not exceeding ten miles square) as may, by cession of particular states, and the acceptance of Congress, become the Seat of the Government of the United States, and to exercise like authority over all places purchased by the consent of the legislature of the state in which the same shall be, for the erection of forts, magazines, arsenals, dockyards, and other needful buildings; - and

(18) To make all laws which shall be necessary and proper for carrying into execution the foregoing powers, and all other powers vested by this Constitution in the Government of the United States, or in any Department or Officer thereof.

Section 9. (1) The migration or importation of such persons as any of the states now existing shall think proper to admit, shall not be prohibited by the Congress prior to the year one thousand eight hundred and eight, but a tax or duty may be imposed on such importation, not exceeding ten dollars for each person.

(2) The privilege of the writ of habeas corpus shall not be suspended, unless when in cases of rebellion or invasion the public safety may require it.

(3) No bill of attainder or ex post facto law shall be passed.

(4) No capitation, or other direct, tax shall be laid, unless in proportion to the census or enumeration herein before directed to be taken.

(5) No tax or duty shall be laid on articles exported from any state.

(6) No preference shall be given by any regulation of commerce or revenue to the ports of one state over those of another: nor shall vessels bound to, or from, one state be obliged to enter, clear, or pay duties in another.

(7) No money shall be drawn from the Treasury, but in consequence of appropriations made by law; and a regular statement and account of the receipts and expenditures of all public money shall be published from time to time.

(8) No title of nobility shall be granted by the United States: and no person holding any office of profit or trust under them, shall, without the consent of the Congress, accept of any present, emolument, office, or title, of any kind whatever, from any King, Prince, or foreign State.

Section 10. (1) No state shall enter into any treaty, alliance, or confederation; grant letters of marque and reprisal; coin money; emit bills of credit; make any thing but gold and silver coin a tender in payment of debts; pass any bill of attainder, ex post facto law, or law impairing the obligation of contracts, or grant any title of nobility.

(2) No state shall, without the consent of the Congress, lay any imposts or duties on imports or exports, except what may be absolutely necessary for executing its inspection laws: and the net produce of all duties and imposts, laid by any state on imports or exports, shall be for the use of

the Treasury of the United States; and all such laws shall be subject to the revision and control of the Congress.

(3) No state shall, without the consent of Congress, lay any duty of tonnage, keep troops, or ships of war in time of peace, enter into any agreement or compact with another state, or with a foreign power, or engage in war, unless actually invaded, or in such imminent danger as will not admit of delay.

ARTICLE II

Section 1. (1) The executive power shall be vested in a President of the United States of America. He shall hold his office during the term of four years, and, together with the Vice President, chosen for the same term, be elected, as follows:

(2) Each state shall appoint, in such manner as the legislature thereof may direct, a number of electors, equal to the whole number of Senators and Representatives to which the state may be entitled in the Congress; but no Senator or Representative, or person holding an office of trust or profit under the United States, shall be appointed an Elector.

(3) The electors shall meet in their respective states, and vote by ballot for two persons, of whom one at least shall not be an inhabitant of the same state with themselves. And they shall make a list of all the persons voted for, and of the number of votes for each; which list they shall sign and certify, and transmit sealed to the Seat of the Government of the United States, directed to the President of the Senate. The President of the Senate shall, in the presence of the Senate and House of Representatives,

open all the certificates, and the votes shall then be counted. The person having the greatest number of votes shall be the President, if such number be a majority of the whole number of electors appointed; and if there be more than one who have such majority, and have an equal number of votes, then the House of Representatives shall immediately choose by ballot one of them for President; and if no person have a majority, then from the five highest on the list the said House shall in like manner choose the President. But in choosing the President, the votes shall be taken by states the representation from each state having one vote; a quorum for this purpose shall consist of a member or members from two-thirds of the states, and a majority of all the states shall be necessary to a choice. In every case, after the choice of the President, the person having the greater number of votes of the electors shall be the Vice President. But if there should remain two or more who have equal votes, the Senate shall choose from them by ballot the Vice President.

(4) The Congress may determine the time of choosing the Electors, and the day on which they shall give their votes; which day shall be the same throughout the United States.

(5) No person except a natural born citizen, or a citizen of the United States, at the time of the adoption of this Constitution, shall be eligible to the Office of President; neither shall any person be eligible to that Office who shall not have attained to the age of thirty-five years, and been fourteen years a resident within the United States.

(6) In case of the removal of the President from Office, or of his death, resignation or inability to discharge the powers and duties of the said Office, the same shall devolve on the Vice President, and the Congress may by law

provide for the case of removal, death, resignation or inability, both of the President and Vice President, declaring what Officer shall then act as President, and such Officer shall act accordingly, until the disability be removed, or a President shall be elected.

(7) The President shall, at stated times, receive for his services, a compensation, which shall neither be increased nor diminished during the period for which he shall have been elected, and he shall not receive within that period any other emolument from the United States, or any of them.

(8) Before he enter on the execution of his office, he shall take the following oath or affirmation: "I do solemnly swear (or affirm) that I will faithfully execute the Office of President of the United States, and will to the best of my ability, preserve, protect and defend the Constitution of the United States."

Section 2. (1) The President shall be Commander in Chief of the Army and Navy of the United States, and of the militia of the several states, when called into the actual service of the United States; he may require the opinion, in writing, of the principal Officer in each of the Executive Departments, upon any subject relating to the duties of their respective Offices, and he shall have power to grant reprieves and pardons for offenses against the United States, except in cases of impeachment.

(2) He shall have power, by and with the advice and consent of the Senate to make treaties, provided two-thirds of the Senators present concur; and he shall nominate, and by and with the advice and consent of the Senate, shall appoint Ambassadors, other public Ministers and Consuls,

Judges of the supreme Court, and all other Officers of the United States, whose appointments are not herein otherwise provided for, and which shall be established by law; but the Congress may by law vest the appointment of such inferior Officers, as they think proper, in the President alone, in the courts of law, or in the heads of departments.

(3) The President shall have power to fill up all vacancies that may happen during the recess of the Senate, by granting commissions which shall expire at the end of their next session.

Section 3. He shall from time to time give to the Congress information of the State of the Union, and recommend to their consideration such measures as he shall judge necessary and expedient; he may, on extraordinary occasions, convene both Houses, or either of them, and in case of disagreement between them, with respect to the time of adjournment, he may adjourn them to such time as he shall think proper; he shall receive Ambassadors and other public Ministers; he shall take care that the laws be faithfully executed, and shall commission all the Officers of the United States.

Section 4. The President, Vice President and all civil Officers of the United States, shall be removed from office on impeachment for, and conviction of, treason, bribery, or other high crimes and misdemeanors.

ARTICLE III

Section 1. The judicial power of the United States, shall be vested in one supreme Court, and in such inferior courts as the Congress may from time to time ordain and establish. The Judges, both of the supreme and inferior courts, shall hold their Offices during good behaviour, and shall, at stated times, receive for their services a compensation, which shall not be diminished during their continuance in office.

Section 2. (1) The judicial power shall extend to all cases, in law and equity, arising under this Constitution, the laws of the United States, and treaties made, or which shall be made, under their authority; - to all cases affecting Ambassadors, other public Ministers and Consuls; - to all cases of admiralty and maritime jurisdiction; - to controversies to which the United States shall be a party; - to controversies between two or more states; - between a state and citizens of another state; - between citizens of different states; - between citizens of the same state claiming lands under the grants of different states, and between a state, or the citizens thereof, and foreign states, citizens or subjects.

(2) In all cases affecting Ambassadors, other public Ministers and Consuls, and those in which a state shall be a party, the supreme Court shall have original jurisdiction. In all the other cases before mentioned, the supreme Court shall have appellate jurisdiction, both as to law and fact, with such exceptions, and under such regulations as the Congress shall make.

(3) The trial of all crimes, except in cases of impeachment, shall be by jury; and such trial shall be held in the state where the said crimes shall have been committed; but when not committed within any state, the trial shall be at such place or places as the Congress may by law have directed.

Section 3. (1) Treason against the United States, shall consist only in levying war against them, or, in adhering to their enemies, giving them aid and comfort. No person shall be convicted of treason unless on the testimony of two witnesses to the same overt act, or on confession in open Court.

(2) The Congress shall have power to declare the punishment of treason, but no Attainder of Treason shall work corruption of blood, or forfeiture except during the life of the person attainted.

ARTICLE IV

Section 1. Full faith and credit shall be given in each state to the public acts, records, and judicial proceedings of every other state. And the Congress may by general laws prescribe the manner in which such acts, records and proceedings shall be proved, and the effect thereof.

Section 2. (1) The citizens of each state shall be entitled to all privileges and immunities of citizens in the several states.

(2) A person charged in any state with treason, felony, or other crime, who shall flee from justice, and be found in another state, shall on demand of the executive authority of the state from which he fled, be delivered up, to be removed to the state having jurisdiction of the crime.

(3) No person held to service or labor in one state, under the laws thereof, escaping into another, shall, in consequence of any law or regulation therein, be discharged from such service or labor, but shall be delivered up on

claim of the party to whom such service or labor may be due.

Section 3. (1) New states may be admitted by the Congress into this union; but no new state shall be formed or erected within the jurisdiction of any other state; nor any state be formed by the junction of two or more states, or parts of states, without the consent of the legislatures of the states concerned as well as of the Congress.

(2) The Congress shall have power to dispose of and make all needful rules and regulations respecting the territory or other property belonging to the United States; and nothing in this Constitution shall be so construed as to prejudice any claims of the United States, or of any particular state.

Section 4. The United States shall guarantee to every state in this union a Republican form of government, and shall protect each of them against invasion; and on application of the legislature, or of the executive (when the legislature cannot be convened) against domestic violence.

ARTICLE V

The Congress, whenever two-thirds of both Houses shall deem it necessary, shall propose amendments to this Constitution, or, on the application of the legislatures of two-thirds of the several states, shall call a convention for proposing amendments, which, in either case, shall be valid to all intents and purposes, as part of this constitution, when ratified by the legislatures of three-fourths of the several states, or by conventions in three-fourths thereof, as the one or the other mode of ratification may be proposed by the Congress; provided that no amendment which may be made prior to the year one thousand eight hundred and eight shall in any manner affect the first and fourth clauses in the Ninth Section of the first Article; and that no state, without its consent, shall be deprived of its equal suffrage in the Senate.

ARTICLE VI

(1) All debts contracted and engagements entered into, before the adoption of this Constitution shall be as valid against the United States under this Constitution, as under the Confederation.

(2) This Constitution, and the laws of the United States which shall be made in pursuance thereof; and all treaties made, or which shall be made, under the authority of the United States, shall be the supreme law of the land; and the Judges in every state shall be bound thereby, any thing in the Constitution or laws of any state to the contrary notwithstanding.

(3) The Senators and Representatives before mentioned, and the Members of the several State Legislatures, and all executive and judicial Officers, both of the United States and of the several states, shall be bound by oath or affirmation, to support this Constitution; but no religious test shall ever be required as a qualification to any office or public trust under the United States.

ARTICLE VII

The ratification of the Conventions of nine states shall be sufficient for the establishment of this Constitution between the states so ratifying the same.

AMENDMENT I (1791)

Congress shall make no law respecting an establishment of religion, or prohibiting the free exercise thereof; or abridging the freedom of speech, or of the press; or the right of the people peaceably to assemble, and to petition the Government for a redress of grievances.

AMENDMENT II (1791)

A well regulated Militia, being necessary to the security of a free state, the right of the people to keep and bear arms, shall not be infringed.

AMENDMENT III (1791)

No soldier shall, in time of peace be quartered in any house, without the consent of the owner, nor in time of war, but in a manner to be prescribed by law.

AMENDMENT IV (1791)

The right of the people to be secure in their persons, houses, papers, and effects, against unreasonable searches and seizures, shall not be violated, and no warrants shall issue, but upon probable cause, supported by oath or affirmation, and particularly describing the place to be searched, and the persons or things to be seized.

AMENDMENT V (1791)

No person shall be held to answer for a capital, or otherwise infamous crime, unless on a presentment or indictment of a Grand Jury, except in cases arising in the land or naval forces, or in the Militia, when in actual service in time of war or public danger; nor shall any person be subject for the same offense to be twice put in jeopardy of life or limb; nor shall be compelled in any criminal case to be a witness against himself, nor be deprived of life, liberty, or property, without due process of law; nor shall private property be taken for public use, without just compensation.

AMENDMENT VI (1791)

In all criminal prosecutions, the accused shall enjoy the right to a speedy and public trial, by an impartial jury of the state and district wherein the crime shall have been committed, which district shall have been previously ascertained by law, and to be informed of the nature and cause of the accusation; to be confronted with the witnesses against him; to have compulsory process for obtaining witnesses in his favor, and to have the assistance of counsel for his defense.

AMENDMENT VII (1791)

In suits at common law, where the value in controversy shall exceed twenty dollars, the right of trial by jury shall be preserved, and no fact tried by jury, shall be otherwise re-examined in any court of the United States, than according to the rules of the common law.

AMENDMENT VIII (1791)

Excessive bail shall not be required, nor excessive fines imposed, nor cruel and unusual punishments inflicted.

AMENDMENT IX (1791)

The enumeration in the Constitution, of certain rights, shall not be construed to deny or disparage others retained by the people.

AMENDMENT X (1791)

The powers not delegated to the United States by the Constitution, nor prohibited by it to the States, are reserved to the States respectively, or to the people.

AMENDMENT XI (1798)

The judicial power of the United States shall not be construed to extend to any suit in law or equity, commenced or prosecuted against one of the United States by citizens of another state, or by citizens or subjects of any foreign state.

AMENDMENT XII (1804)

The Electors shall meet in their respective states and vote by ballot for President and Vice-President, one of whom, at least, shall not be an inhabitant of the same state with themselves; they shall name in their ballots the person voted for as President, and in distinct ballots the person voted for as Vice-President, and they shall make distinct lists of all persons voted for as President, and of all persons voted for as Vice-President, and of the number of votes for each, which lists they shall sign and certify, and transmit sealed to the seat of the government of the United States, directed to the President of the Senate; - the President of the Senate shall, in the presence of the Senate and House of Representatives, open all the certificates and the votes shall then be counted; - the person having the greatest number of votes for President, shall be the President, if such number be a majority of the whole number of electors appointed; and if no person have such majority, then from the persons having the highest numbers not exceeding three on the list of those voted for as President, the House of Representatives shall choose immediately, by ballot, the President. But in choosing the President, the votes shall be taken by states, the representation from each state having one vote; a quorum for this purpose shall consist of a member or members from two-thirds of the states, and a majority of all the states shall be necessary to a choice. And if the House of Representatives shall not choose a President whenever the right of choice shall devolve upon them before the fourth day of March next following, then the Vice-President shall act as President, as in the case of the death or other constitutional disability of the President. - The person having the greatest number of votes as Vice-President, shall be the Vice-President, if such number be a majority of the whole number of Electors appointed, and if no person have a majority, then from the two highest numbers on the list, the Senate shall choose the Vice-President; a quorum for the purpose shall consist of two-thirds of the whole number of Senators, and a majority of the whole number shall be necessary to a choice. But no person constitutionally ineligible to the office of President shall be eligible to that of Vice-President of the United States.

AMENDMENT XIII (1865)

Section 1. Neither slavery nor involuntary servitude, except as a punishment for crime whereof the party shall have been duly convicted, shall exist within the United States, or any place subject to their jurisdiction.

Section 2. Congress shall have power to enforce this article by appropriate legislation.

AMENDMENT XIV (1868)

Section 1. All persons born or naturalized in the United States, and subject to the jurisdiction thereof, are citizens of the United States and of the state wherein they reside. No state shall make or enforce any law which shall abridge the privileges or immunities of citizens of the United States; nor shall any state deprive any person of life, liberty, or property, without due process of law; nor deny to any person within its jurisdiction the equal protection of the laws.

Section 2. Representatives shall be apportioned among the several states according to their respective numbers, counting the whole number of persons in each State excluding Indians not taxed. But when the right to vote at any election for the choice of electors for President and Vice President of the United States, Representatives in Congress, the Executive and Judicial officers of a state, or the members of the Legislature thereof, is denied to any of the male inhabitants of such state, being twenty-one years of age, and citizens of the United States, or in any way abridged, except for participation in rebellion, or other crime, the basis of representation therein shall be reduced in the proportion which the number of such male citizens shall bear to the whole number of male citizens twenty-one years of age in such state.

Section 3. No person shall be a Senator or Representative in Congress, or elector of President and Vice President, or hold any office, civil or military, under the United States, or under any state, who having previously taken an oath, as a member of Congress, or as an officer of the United States, or as a member of any state legislature, or as an executive or judicial officer of any state, to support the Constitution of the United States, shall have engaged in insurrection or rebellion against the same, or given aid or comfort to the enemies thereof. But Congress may by a vote of two-thirds of each House, remove such disability.

Section 4. The validity of the public debt of the United States, authorized by law, including debts incurred for payment of pensions and bounties for services in suppressing insurrection or rebellion, shall not be questioned. But neither the United States nor any state shall assume or pay any debt or obligation incurred in aid of insurrection or rebellion against the United States, or any claim for the loss or emancipation of any slave; but all such debts, obligations and claims shall be held illegal and void.

Section 5. The Congress shall have power to enforce, by appropriate legislation, the provisions of this article.

AMENDMENT XV (1870)

Section 1. The right of citizens of the United States to vote shall not be denied or abridged by the United States or by any state on account of race, color, or previous condition of servitude.

Section 2. The Congress shall have power to enforce this article by appropriate legislation.

AMENDMENT XVI (1913)

The Congress shall have power to lay and collect taxes on incomes, from whatever source derived, without apportionment among the several states, and without regard to any census or enumeration.

AMENDMENT XVII (1913)

(1) The Senate of the United States shall be composed of two Senators from each state, elected by the people thereof, for six years; and each Senator shall have one vote. The electors in each State shall have the qualifications requisite for electors of the most numerous branch of the state legislatures.

(2) When vacancies happen in the representation of any state in the Senate, the executive authority of such state shall issue writs of election to fill such vacancies: *provided*, that the legislature of any state may empower the executive thereof to make temporary appointments until the people fill the vacancies by election as the legislature may direct.

(3) This amendment shall not be so construed as to affect the election or term of any Senator chosen before it becomes valid as part of the Constitution.

AMENDMENT XVIII (1919)

Section 1. After one year from the ratification of this article the manufacture, sale, or transportation of intoxicating liquors within, the importation thereof into, or the exportation thereof from the United States and all territory subject to the jurisdiction thereof for beverage purposes is hereby prohibited.

Section 2. The Congress and the several states shall have concurrent power to enforce this article by appropriate legislation.

Section 3. This article shall be inoperative unless it shall have been ratified as an amendment to the Constitution by the legislatures of the several states, as provided in the Constitution, within seven years from the date of the submission hereof to the states by the Congress.

AMENDMENT XIX (1920)

(1) The right of citizens of the United States to vote shall not be denied or abridged by the United States or by any state on account of sex.

(2) Congress shall have power to enforce this article by appropriate legislation.

AMENDMENT XX (1933)

Section 1. The terms of the President and Vice President shall end at noon on the 20th day of January, and the terms of Senators and Representatives at noon on the 3d day of January, of the years in which such terms would have ended if this article had not been ratified; and the terms of their successors shall then begin.

Section 2. The Congress shall assemble at least once in every year, and such meeting shall begin at noon on the 3d day of January, unless they shall by law appoint a different day.

Section 3. If, at the time fixed for the beginning of the term of the President, the President elect shall have died, the Vice President elect shall become President. If the President shall not have been chosen before the time fixed for the beginning of his term, or if the President elect shall have failed to qualify, then the Vice President elect shall act as President until a President shall have qualified; and the Congress may by law provide for the case wherein neither a President elect nor a Vice President elect shall have qualified, declaring who shall then act as President, or the manner in which one who is to act shall be selected, and such person shall act accordingly until a President or Vice President shall have qualified.

Section 4. The Congress may by law provide for the case of the death of any of the persons from whom the House of Representatives may choose a President whenever the right of choice shall have devolved upon them, and for the case of the death of any of the persons from whom the Senate may choose a Vice President whenever the right of choice shall have devolved upon them.

Section 5. Sections 1 and 2 shall take effect on the 15th day of October following the ratification of this article.

Section 6. This article shall be inoperative unless it shall have been ratified as an amendment to the Constitution by the legislatures of three-fourths of the several states within seven years from the date of its submission.

AMENDMENT XXI (1933)

Section 1. The eighteenth article of amendment to the Constitution of the United States is hereby repealed.

Section 2. The transportation or importation into any state, territory, or possession of the United States for delivery or use therein of intoxicating liquors, in violation of the laws thereof, is hereby prohibited.

Section 3. This article shall be inoperative unless it shall have been ratified as an amendment to the Constitution by conventions in the several states, as provided in the Constitution, within seven years from the date of the submission hereof to the states by the Congress.

AMENDMENT XXII (1951)

Section 1. No person shall be elected to the office of the President more than twice, and no person who has held the office of President, or acted as President, for more than two years of a term to which some other person was elected President shall be elected to the office of President more than once. But this Article shall not apply to any person holding the office of President when this Article was proposed by the Congress, and shall not prevent any person who may be holding the office of President, or acting as President, during the term within which this Article becomes operative from holding the office of President or acting as President during the remainder of such term.

Section 2. This article shall be inoperative unless it shall have been ratified as an amendment to the Constitution by the legislatures of three-fourths of the several states within seven years from the date of its submission to the states by the Congress.

AMENDMENT XXIII (1961)

Section 1. The District constituting the seat of Government of the United States shall appoint in such manner as the Congress may direct:

A number of electors of President and Vice President equal to the whole number of Senators and Representatives in Congress to which the District would be entitled if it were a state, but in no event more than the least populous state; they shall be in addition to those appointed by the states, but they shall be considered, for the purposes of the election of President and Vice President, to be electors appointed by a state; and they shall meet in the District and perform such duties as provided by the twelfth article of amendment.

Section 2. The Congress shall have power to enforce this article by appropriate legislation.

AMENDMENT XXIV (1964)

Section 1. The right of citizens of the United States to vote in any primary or other election for President or Vice President, for electors for President or Vice President, or for Senator or Representative in Congress, shall not be denied or abridged by the United States, or any state by reason of failure to pay any poll tax or other tax.

Section 2. The Congress shall have power to enforce this article by appropriate legislation.

AMENDMENT XXV (1967)

Section 1. In case of the removal of the President from office or of his death or resignation, the Vice President shall become President.

Section 2. Whenever there is a vacancy in the office of the Vice President, the President shall nominate a Vice President who shall take office upon confirmation by a majority vote of both Houses of Congress.

Section 3. Whenever the President transmits to the President pro tempore of the Senate and the Speaker of the House of Representatives his written declaration that he is unable to discharge the powers and duties of his office, and until he transmits to them a written declaration to the contrary, such powers and duties shall be discharged by the Vice President as Acting President.

Section 4. Whenever the Vice President and a majority of either the principal officers of the executive departments or of such other body as Congress may by law provide, transmit to the President pro tempore of the Senate and the Speaker of the House of Representatives their written declaration that the President is unable to discharge the powers and duties of his office, the Vice President shall immediately assume the powers and duties of the office as Acting President.

Thereafter, when the President transmits to the President pro tempore of the Senate and the Speaker of the House of Representatives his written declaration that no inability exists, he shall resume the powers and duties of his office unless the Vice President and a majority of either the principal officers of the executive department or of such other body as Congress may by law provide, transmit within four days to the President pro tempore of the Senate and the Speaker of the House of Representatives their written declaration and the President is unable to discharge the powers and duties of his office. Thereupon Congress shall decide the issue, assembling within forty-eight hours for that purpose if not in session. If the Congress, within twenty-one days after receipt of the latter written declaration, or, if Congress is not in session, within twenty-one days after Congress is required to assemble, determines by two-thirds vote of both Houses that the President is unable to discharge the power and duties of his office, the Vice President shall continue to discharge the same as Acting President; otherwise, the President shall resume the powers and duties of his office.

AMENDMENT XXVI (1971)

Section 1. The right of citizens of the United States, who are eighteen years of age or older, to vote shall not be denied or abridged by the United States or by any state on account of age.

Section 2. The Congress shall have power to enforce this article by appropriate legislation.

AMENDMENT XXVII (1992)

No law, varying the compensation for the services of the Senators and Representatives, shall take effect, until an election of Representatives shall have intervened.

BIBLIOGRAPHY

Alcorn, Randy C. *Is Rescuing Right? Breaking the Law to Save the Unborn.* Downers Grove, IL: InterVarsity Press, 1990.

Allison, Loraine. *Finding Peace After Abortion.* St. Meinrad, IN: Abbey Press, 1990.

Anderson, Richard. *Abortion Pro & Con.* Los Angeles, CA: Right to Life League, 1977.

Baird, Robert M. and Stuart E. Rosenbaum, Editors. *The Ethics of Abortion: The Continuing Debate.* Buffalo, NY: Prometheus Books, 1989.

Baker, Don. *Beyond Choice: The Abortion Story No One Is Telling.* Portland, OR: Multnomah Press, 1985.

Banks, Bill and Sue Banks. *Ministering to Abortion's Aftermath.* Kirkwood, MO: Impact Books, 1982.

Barry, Robert L. *Medical Ethics: Essays on Abortion and Euthanasia.* Billings, MT: Peter Lang Publications, 1989.

Baulieu, Etienne-Emile and Mort Rosenblum. *The "Abortion Pill": RU-486, A Woman's Choice.* New York, NY: Simon & Schuster, 1991.

Batchelor, Edward, Jr., Editor. *Abortion: The Moral Issues.* New York, NY: Pilgrim Press, 1982.

Berger, G. and W. Brenner, Editors. *Second Trimester Abortion.* Kluwer, N.V.: Kluwer Academic Publishers, 1981.

Bonavoglia, Angela, Editor. *The Choices We Made: 25 Women and Men Speak Out About Abortion.* New York, NY: Random House, 1991.

Bondesor, William B. and H. Tristram Engelhardt. *Abortion and the Status of the Fetus.* Kluwer, N.V.: Kluwer Academic Publishers, 1983.

Braun, Eric A. and LauraLee Gaudio. *Living with Your Choice: An Inner Healing for Abortion.* Sea Cliff, NY: Purelight, 1990.

Briscoe, Clarence C. *Abortion: The Emotional Issue.* Pittsburgh, PA: Dorrance Publishing Co., 1984.

Browder, Clifford. *The Wickedest Woman in New York: Madame Restelle, The Abortionist.* Hamden, CT: Archon Books, 1988.

Brown, Harold O.J. *The Bible on Abortion.* Minneapolis, MN: Free Church Publications, 1977.

Butler, J. Douglas and David F. Walbert, Editors. *Abortion, Medicine and the Law.* New York, NY: Facts on File, 1986.

Callahan, Sidney and Daniel Callahan. *Abortion: Understanding Differences.* New York, NY: Plenum Press, 1984.

Cohen, M., et al., Editors. *Rights and Wrongs of Abortion.* Princeton, NJ: Princeton University Press, 1974.

Condit, Celeste Michelle. *Decoding Abortion Rhetoric: Communicating Social Change.* Chicago: University of Illinois Press, 1990.

Connery, John. *Abortion: The Development of the Roman Catholic Perspective.* Chicago, IL: Loyola University Press, 1977.

Corsaro, Maria and Carole Korzeniowsky. *A Woman's Guide to Safe Abortion.* New York, NY: Holt, Rinehart & Winston, 1983.

Costa, Maria. *Abortion: A Reference Handbook.* Santa Barbara, CA: ABC-CLIO, 1991.

Coughlan, Michael J. *The Vatican, the Law and the Human Embryo.* Iowa City, IA: University of Iowa Press, 1990.

Cozic, Charles and Tracey Tipp, Editors. *Abortion: Opposing Viewpoints.* San Diego, CA: Greenhaven Press, 1991.

Cunningham, Paige C., et al., Editors. *Abortion and the Constitution: Reversing Roe v. Wade Through the Courts.* Washington, DC: Georgetown University Press, 1987.

Curtzinger, G. *Abortion, Person as Thing.* Mansfield, TX: Latitudes Press, 1988.

Davis, John J. *Abortion and the Christian.* Phillipsburg, NJ: Presbyterian & Reformed Publishing Co., 1984.

Devereux, George. *A Study of Abortion in Primitive Societies.* Madison, CT: International Universities Press, 1976.

Doerr, Edd and James W. Prescott, Editors. *Abortion Rights and Fetal "Personhood."* Long Beach, CA: Centerline Press, 1990.

Emmens, Carol A. *The Abortion Controversy.* New York, NY: Julian Messner, 1987.

Erdahl, Lowell O. *Pro-Life, Pro-Peace: Life Affirming Alternatives to Abortion, War, Mercy Killing, and the Death Penalty.* Minneapolis, MN: Augsburg Fortress Publishers, 1986.

Faux, Marian. *Crusaders: Voices From the Abortion Front.* Secausus, NJ: Carol Pub. Group, 1990.

Faux, Marion. *Roe v. Wade: The Story of the Landmark Supreme Court Decision That Made Abortion Legal.* New York, NY: Macmillan, 1988.

Feinberg, Joel, Editor. *The Problem of Abortion.* Belmont, CA: Wadsworth Publishing Co., 1984.

Ferraro, Barbara, and Patricia Hussey, with Jane O'Reilly. *No Turning Back: Two Nuns' Battle With the Vatican over Women's Right to Choose.* New York, NY: Poseidon Press, 1990.

Flanders, Carl N. *Abortion.* New York, NY: Facts on File, 1991.

Forelle, Helen. *If Men Got Pregnant, Abortion Would be a Sacrament.* Sioux Falls, SD: Tesseract Publications, 1991.

Fowler, Paul. *Abortion: Toward an Evangelical Consensus.* Portland, OR: Multnomah Press, 1987.

Francke, Linda Bird. *The Ambivalence of Abortion.* New York, NY: Random House, 1978.

Francome, Colin. *Abortion Freedom: A Worldwide Movement.* New York, NY: Unwin Hyman, 1984.

Gardner, Joy. *A Difficult Decision: A Compassionate Book About Abortion.* Trumansburg, NY: Crossing Press, 1986.

Garfield, Jay L. and Patricia Hennessey, Editors. *Abortion: Moral and Legal Perspectives.* Amherst, MA: University of Massachusetts Press, 1985.

Gaylor, Anne N. *Abortion is a Blessing.* New York, NY: Psychological Dimensions, 1976.

Ginsburg, Faye D. *Contested Lives: The Abortion Debate in an American Community.* Berkeley: University of California Press, 1989.

Glessner, Thomas A. *Achieving an Abortion-Free America by 2001.* Portland, OR: Multnomah Press, 1990.

Goldstein, Robert D. *Mother-Love and Abortion: A Legal Interpretation.* Berkeley, CA: University of California Press, 1988.

Grady, John L. *Abortion: Yes or No?* Rockford, IL: TAN Books Pubs., 1968.

Grenier-Sweet, Gail, Editor. *Pro-Life Feminism: Different Voices.* Lewiston, NY: Life Cycle Books, 1985.

Hall, Robert E., Editor. *Abortion in a Changing World.* NY: Columbia University Press, 1970.

Harris, Harry. *Prenatal Diagnosis and Selective Abortion.* Cambridge, MA: Harvard University Press, 1975.

Harrison, Beverly Wildung. *Our Right to Choose: Toward a New Ethic of Abortion.* Boston: Beacon Press, 1983.

Harrison, Maureen, and Steve Gilbert. *Landmark Decisions of the United States Supreme Court, Vol. I.* Beverly Hills, CA: Excellent Books, 1991.

Hern, Warren M. *Abortion Practice.* Boulder, CO: Alpenglo Graphics, 1990.

Hern, Warren M. *Abortion Services Handbook.* Durant, OK: Creative Informatics, 1978.

Hertz, Sue. *Caught in the Crossfire: A Year on Abortion's Front Line.* New York, NY: Prentice Hall, 1991.

Horan, Dennis J., Edward R. Grant and Paige C. Cunningham, Editors. *Abortion and the Constitution: Reversing Roe v. Wade Through the Courts.* Washington, DC: Georgetown University Press, 1987.

Howe, Louise K. *Moments on Maple Avenue: The Reality of Abortion.* New York, NY: Warner Books, 1986.

Ide, Arthur F. *Abortion Handbook: History, Clinical Practice and Psychology of Abortion.* Las Colinas, TX: Liberal Press, 1987.

Imber, Jonathan B. *Abortion and the Private Practice of Medicine.* New Haven, CT: Yale University Press, 1986.

Joyce, Robert and Mary R. Joyce. *Let's Be Born: The Inhumanity of Abortion.* Chicago, IL: Franciscan Herald Press, 1976.

Jung, Patricia Beattie and Thomas A. Shannon, Editors. *Abortion and Catholicism: The American Debate.* New York, NY: Crossroad, 1988.

Justus, Adalu. *Dear Mommy, Please Don't Kill Me.* Hesperia, CA: Silo Pubs., 1986.

Keemer, Edgar B. *Confessions of a Pro-Life Abortionist.* Detroit, MI: Vinco Press, 1980.

Keirse, M. and Bennebroek J. Gravenhorst, Editors. *Second Trimester Pregnancy Termination.* Kluwer, N.V.: Kluwer Academic Publishers, 1982.

Kenyon, Edwin. *The Dilemma of Abortion.* Winchester, MA: Faber & Faber, 1986.

Kerr, Fred W. *Ninety Days for Life: The Jailhouse Journal of "Operation Rescue" Internee, Fred W. Kerr.* Hannibal, MO: Hannibal Books, 1989.

Koerbel, Pam. *Does Anyone Else Feel Like I Do?* New York, NY: Doubleday, 1990.

Kogan, Barry S., Editor. *A Time to be Born and a Time to Die: The Ethics of Choice.* Hawthorne, NY: Aldine de Gruyter, 1991.

Krason, Stephen M. *Abortion: Politics, Morality, and the Constitution: A Critical Study of Roe v., Wade and Doe v. Bolton and a Basis for Change.* Lanham, MD: University Press of America, 1984.

Lader, Lawrence. *Abortion.* New York, NY: Macmillan, 1966.

Lader, Lawrence. *RU-486: The Pill That Could End the Abortion Wars and Why American Women Don't Have It.* New York, NY: Addison-Wesley, 1991.

Lee, Nancy H. *Search for an Abortionist.* Chicago: University of Chicago Press, 1969.

Legge, Jerome S., Jr. *Abortion Policy: An Evaluation of the Consequences for Maternal and Infant Health.* Albany, NY: State University of New York Press, 1985.

Luker, Kristin. *Abortion and the Politics of Motherhood.* Berkeley: University of California Press, 1984.

Luker, Kristin. *Taking Chances: Abortion and the Decision Not to Contracept.* Berkeley: University of California Press, 1975.

Lunneborg, Patricia W. *A Positive Decision.* New York, NY: Bergin & Garvey, 1992.

McCarthy, John F. *In Defense of Human Life.* Houston, TX: Lumen Christi Press, 1970.

McCartney, James J. *Unborn Persons: Pope John Paul II and the Abortion Debate.* New York, NY: Peter Lang Publishing, 1988.

McDonnell, Kathleen. *Not An Easy Choice: A Feminist Re-examines Abortion.* Boston: South End Press, 1984.

Mall, David. *In Good Conscience: Abortion and Moral Necessity.* Columbus, OH: Kairos Books, 1982.

Mannion, Michael T. *Abortion and Healing: A Cry to Be Whole.* Kansas City, MO: Sheed & Ward, 1986.

Melton, Gary B., Editor. *Adolescent Abortion: Psychological and Legal Issues.* Lincoln, NE: University of Nebraska Press, 1986.

Meyers, David W. *The Human Body and the Law.* Palo Alto: Stanford University Press, 1991.

Miley, LaVerne. *Abortion: Right or Wrong?* Nashville, TN: Randall House Publications, 1981.

Mohr, James C. *Abortion in America: The Origins and Evolution of National Policy, 1800-1900.* New York, NY: Oxford University Press, 1978.

Muldoon, Maureen, Editor. *Abortion: An Annotated In-dexed Bibliography.* Lewiston, NY: Edwin Mellen Press, 1980.

Nathanson, Sue. *Soul Crisis: One Woman's Journey Through Abortion to Renewal.* New York, NY: New American Library, 1989.

National Issues Forum Staff. *The Battle Over Abortion: Seeking Common Ground in a Divided Nation.* Du-buque, IA: Kendall-Hunt Publishing Co., 1990.

Newman, Sidney H., et al., Editors. *Abortion, Obtained and Denied: Research Aproaches.* New York, NY: Popu-lation Council, 1971.

Noonan, John T., Jr. *A Private Choice: Abortion in Amer-ica in the Seventies.* New York, NY: Free Press, 1979.

Norrie, Kenneth M. *Family Planning and the Law. Santa Cruz, CA: Gower Publishing Co., 1991.*

Odell, Catherine and William Odell. *The First Human Right: A Pro-Life Primer.* Huntington, IN: Our Sunday Visitor, 1983.

Paige, Connie. *The Right to Lifers: Who They Are, How They Operate, Where They Get Their Money.* New York, NY: Summit Books, 1983.

Pastuszek, Eric J. *Is the Fetus Human?* Avon, NJ: Magni-ficat Press, 1991.

Podell, Janet, Editor. *Abortion.* New York, NY: H.W. Wilson Co., 1990.

Powell, John. *Abortion: The Silent Holocaust.* Allen, TX: Tabor Publishing, 1981.

Reardon, David C. *Aborted Women: Silent No More.* Gaithersburg, MD: Human Life International, 1987.

Reisser, Teri K. and Paul Reisser. *Help for Post-Abortion Women.* Grand Rapids, MI: Zondervan Pub. House, 1989.

Reynolds, Brenda M. *Human Abortion: Guide for Medicine, Science and Research.* Washington, DC: ABBE Publishers Association, 1984.

Rice, Charles E. *Beyond Abortion: The Origin and Future of the Secular State.* Chicago, IL: Franciscan Herald Press, 1978.

Rodman, Hyman, et al. *The Abortion Question.* New York, NY: Columbia University Press, 1990.

Rodman, Hyman and Susan H. Lewis. *The Sexual Rights of Adolescents: Competence, Vulnerability, and Parental Control.* New York, NY: Columbia University Press, 1988.

Rosenblatt, Roger. *Life Itself: Abortion in the American Mind.* New York, NY: Random House, 1992.

Saltenberger, Ann. *Every Woman Has a Right to Know the Dangers of Legal Abortion.* Garrisonville, VA: Air-Plus Enterprises, 1983.

Sarvis, Betty and Hyman Rodman. *The Abortion Controversy.* New York, NY: Columbia University Press, 1974.

Sass, Lauren R., Editor. *Abortion: Freedom of Choice and the Right to Life.* New York, NY: Facts on File, 1978.

Scheidler, Joseph M. *Closed: 99 Ways to Stop Abortion.* Westchester, IL: Crossway Books, 1985.

Siegel, Mark A., Nancy R. Jacobs, and Patricia Von Brook, Editors. *Abortion: An Eternal Social and Moral Issue.* Wylie, TX: Information Plus, 1990.

Skolnick, Gary E. *Abortion: Index of Modern Information with Bibliography.* Washington, DC: ABBE Publishers Association, 1988.

Skowronski, Marjory. *Abortion and Alternatives.* Millbrae, CA: Les Femmes Publishers, 1977.

Sloan, Carole M. *Love, Abortion and Adoption of Carole Lovelee Williams.* Washington, DC: ABBE Publishers Association, 1988.

Sloan, Irving J. The Law Governing Abortion, Contraception and Sterilization. New York, NY: Oceana Publications, 1988.

Sloan, R. Bruce and Diana F. Horvitz. *A General Guide to Abortion.* Chicago, IL: Nelson-Hall, 1973.

Speckhard, Anne. *Psycho-Social Stress Following Abortion.* Kansas City, MO: Sheed & Ward, 1987.

Sproul, R.C. *Abortion: A Rational Look at an Emotional Issue.* Colorado Springs, CO: NavPress, 1990.

Steiner, Gilbert Y., Editor. *The Abortion Dispute and the American System.* Washington, DC: Brookings Institution, 1983.

Steinhoff, Patricia G. and Milton Diamond. *Abortion Politics: The Hawaii Experience.* Honolulu, HI: University of Hawaii Press, 1977.

Storer, Horatio R. and Franklin F. Heard. *Criminal Abortion.* Salem, NH: Ayer Co. Publishers, 1974.

Summerhill, Louise. *The Story of Birthright: The Alternative to Abortion.* Libertyville, IL: Prow Books, 1973.

Szumski, Bonnie, Editor. *Abortion: Opposing Viewpoints.* St. Paul, MN: Greenhaven Press, 1986.

Terkel, Susan Neiburg. *Abortion: Facing the Issues.* New York, NY: Watts, 1988.

Tickle, Phyllis, Editor. *Confessing Conscience: Churched Women on Abortion.* Nashville, TN: Abingdon Press, 1990.

Tooley, Michael. *Abortion and Infanticide.* New York, NY: Oxford University Press, 1986.

Tribe, Laurence H. *Abortion: The Clash of Absolutes.* New York, NY: Norton, 1990.

Wardle, Lynn D. *The Abortion Privacy Doctrine: A Compendium and Critique of Federal Abortion Cases.* Buffalo, NY: W.S. Hein & Co., 1980.

Weinberg, Roy D. *Family Planning and the Law.* Dobbs Ferry, NY: Oceana Publications, 1979.

Welton, K.B. *Abortion is Not a Sin: A New-Age Look at an Age-Old Problem.* Dana Point, CA: Pandit Press, 1988.

Wennberg, Robert. *Life in the Balance: Exploring the Abortion Controversy. Grand Rapids, MI: William B. Eerdmans Publishing Co., 1985.*

Whitney, Catherine. *Whole Life? A Balanced, Comprehensive View of Abortion From Its Historical Context to the Current Debate.* New York, NY: W. Morrow, 1991.

Wilt, Judith. *Abortion, Choice, and Contemporary Fiction: The Armageddon of the Maternal Instinct.* Chicago: University of Chicago Press, 1990.

Winden, Lori Van. *The Case Against Abortion: A Logical Argument for Life.* Ligouri, MO: Liguori Publications, 1988.

INDEX

EXCELLENT BOOKS ORDER FORM

(Please xerox this form so it will be available to other readers.)

Please send

_____ copy(ies) of ABORTION DECISIONS: THE 1970's
_____ copy(ies) of ABORTION DECISIONS: THE 1980's
_____ copy(ies) of ABORTION DECISIONS: THE 1990's
_____ copy(ies) of LANDMARK DECISIONS
_____ copy(ies) of LANDMARK DECISIONS II
_____ copy(ies) of LANDMARK DECISIONS III
_____ copy(ies) of THE ADA HANDBOOK

Name: _____

Address: _____

City: _____ **State:** _____ **Zip:** _____

Price: $15.95 for ABORTION DECISIONS: THE 1970's
        $15.95 for ABORTION DECISIONS: THE 1980's
        $15.95 for ABORTION DECISIONS: THE 1990's
        $14.95 for LANDMARK DECISIONS
        $15.95 for LANDMARK DECISIONS II
        $15.95 for LANDMARK DECISIONS III
        $15.95 for THE ADA HANDBOOK

        Add $1 per book for shipping and handling
        California residents add sales tax

OUR GUARANTEE: Any Excellent Book may be returned at any time for any reason and a full refund will be made.

Mail your check or money order to: Excellent Books, Post Office Box 7121, Beverly Hills, California 90212-7121 or call (310) 275-6945